The Millionaire JOURNEY

A Guide for Anyone to Reach Financial Freedom

Patrick M. Green, MBA

Copyright © 2017 Patrick M. Green, MBA.

All rights reserved. No part of this book may be used or reproduced by any means, graphic, electronic, or mechanical, including photocopying, recording, taping or by any information storage retrieval system without the written permission of the author except in the case of brief quotations embodied in critical articles and reviews.

The information, ideas, and suggestions in this book are not intended to render professional advice. Before following any suggestions contained in this book, you should consult your personal accountant or other financial advisor. Neither the author nor the publisher shall be liable or responsible for any loss or damage allegedly arising as a consequence of your use or application of any information or suggestions in this book.

WestBow Press books may be ordered through booksellers or by contacting:

WestBow Press
A Division of Thomas Nelson & Zondervan
1663 Liberty Drive
Bloomington, IN 47403
www.westbowpress.com
1 (866) 928-1240

Because of the dynamic nature of the Internet, any web addresses or links contained in this book may have changed since publication and may no longer be valid. The views expressed in this work are solely those of the author and do not necessarily reflect the views of the publisher, and the publisher hereby disclaims any responsibility for them.

Any people depicted in stock imagery provided by Thinkstock are models, and such images are being used for illustrative purposes only.
Certain stock imagery © Thinkstock.

ISBN: 978-1-5127-9845-6 (sc)
ISBN: 978-1-5127-9847-0 (hc)
ISBN: 978-1-5127-9846-3 (e)

Library of Congress Control Number: 2017912630

Print information available on the last page.

WestBow Press rev. date: 09/08/2017

DEDICATION

I would like to dedicate this book to three different groups of people.

First, I would like to reach every young adult out there who is hearing from the culture that the days are gone when one can go out into the world, make a difference, and also make money! They have been made to believe that they have to choose one or the other and cannot do both. They have also been given a path of least resistance that will cause them to go tens or even hundreds of thousands of dollars in debt in the form of school loans to do either! I am here to tell them that there is a better way! To find it, they will have to forgo normal and instead be extraordinary. The good news is most of the young people I know want to be extraordinary!

Second, this book is written for all hardworking families out there who cannot figure out how to make ends meet, let alone get ahead, or dare to dream about becoming millionaires. These families are like the ones I grew up in—good people who want to do right by their families and their communities, but struggle mightily to do so. My goal is that anyone who reads this book will grab hold of the hope and the plan it contains and use it to lift themselves out of their quagmire, get their legs under them and walk, then run, and finally climb to financial freedom. I strive to show them that it is truly is possible for almost anyone, at almost any age, to become financially free.

Lastly, I penned these words for the people who are doing well financially by most people's standards. They are educated, make good or even great incomes, and have all appearances of being wealthy. They live in beautiful homes, drive expensive cars, wear name-brand clothing and accessories, and take exotic vacations. Under the glittering exterior, however, they are under tremendous bondage. The bondage is caused by the debt that was used to buy the aforementioned educations, homes, cars, clothes, and vacations. It weighs on them like the world on Atlas's shoulders, and they see no hope of ever getting out from under it. They feel like rats in the wheels, running as hard as they can but getting nowhere. They remember the dreams of their youth and long to do something meaningful and leave a legacy. My message to them is they can still do it! It is never too late!

> **Whether you think you can, or whether you think you can't, you're right.**
> —**Henry Ford**

> **If you will live like no one else, later you can live and give like no one else.**
> —**Dave Ramsey**

CONTENTS

Dedication v
Prologue ix
Preface xi
Acknowledgments xiii

Chapter 1:   Step 1: Make Up Your Mind to Go 1
Chapter 2:   Use the Force (Like Luke!) 9
Chapter 3:   Step 2: Get to the Train Station! 19
Chapter 4:   Step 3: Pick a track 35
Chapter 5:   Step 4: Pick a Train 53
Chapter 6:   Step 5: Fuel the Engine 63
Chapter 7:   Keeping on Track (By Always Having an Income) ... 81
Chapter 8:   Step 6: Look at the Landscape 91
Chapter 9:   Explore the World 107
Chapter 10: Step 7: Leave a Legacy 113
Chapter 11: It Is Never Too Late! 125
Chapter 12: It Is Time for Your Journey! 131

Epilogue 135

PROLOGUE

The Little Engine that Could

You remember the children's book by Watty Piper. But do you know the story behind the story?

Watty Piper was not the originator of this tale. First published in the *New York Tribune* on April 8, 1906, the story is attributed to a sermon delivered by the Rev. Charles S. Wing. Here is that version in its entirety:

> In a certain railroad yard, there stood an extremely heavy train that had to be drawn up an unusually heavy grade before it could reach its destination. The superintendent of the yard was not sure what it was best for him to do, so he went up to a large, strong engine and asked, "Can you pull that train over the hill?"
>
> "It is a very heavy train," responded the engine.
>
> He then went to another great engine and asked, "Can you pull that train over the hill?"
>
> "It is a very heavy grade," it replied.
>
> The superintendent was much puzzled, but he turned to still another engine that was spick-and-span new, and he asked it, "Can you pull that train over the hill?"

"I think I can," responded the engine.

So the order was circulated, and the engine was started back so that it might be coupled with the train, and as it went along the rails it kept repeating to itself: "I think I can. I think I can. I think I can."

The coupling was made and the engine began its journey, and all along the level, as it rolled toward the ascent, it kept repeating to itself: "I … think …I can. I …think …I… can. I …think… I …can."

Then it reached the grade, but its voice could still be heard: "I think I can. I … think …I … can. I … think … I … can."

Higher and higher it climbed, and its voice grew fainter and its words came slower:

"I … think … I … can."

It was almost to the top.

"I … think …"

It was at the top.

"I … can."

It passed over the top of the hill and began crawling down the opposite slope.

"I … think … I … can … I… thought … I … could. I …thought … could. I thought I could. I thought I could. I thought I could."

And singing its triumph, it rushed on down toward the valley.

What is so intriguing about this version is not the variation of the story but the context. You see, this sermon was given to Rev. Wing's congregation after they had climbed their own mountain. This sermon was the celebration for the Nordstrand Avenue Methodist Episcopal Church as they had finally paid off the mortgage on the church's property. They were debt-free!

They thought they could, and they did!

If you think you can, you will too!

PREFACE

Personal finance has been an area of interest for me since I was a teenager. The first time I remember thinking about it was when an uncle gave me a share of stock in a bank as a birthday present when I was a teenager. He explained that owning a share of stock is owning a piece of a company. I thought it was so cool that I owned a part of a bank! He further explained how the value of a stock can grow and that by owning stock I could grow wealth without working, but instead let the money I invest in stock work for me.

This lesson was reinforced in early adulthood when my wife and I attended a young-married class at church. They used curriculum from Larry Burkett and Ron Blue that focused on being great money managers, avoiding debt, and establishing a prioritized spending plan, otherwise known as a budget. One of the priorities it suggested was investing. It was a struggle, but even as my wife and I were working three jobs and going to night school, we started a budget and started investing in our mid- to late-twenties.

Flash-forward another twenty-five years and we found ourselves in a place of Financial Freedom that we honestly never dreamed of in our early adult years. We were completely out of debt, including our house, and had a seven-figure nest egg for retirement. The last push toward this freedom was inspired by the writings and teachings of Dave Ramsey and his team at Ramsey Solutions.

In between, there have been many other teachers and leaders who have inspired me to achieve more, serve more, love more, and be more than I ever would have thought to do without their wisdom and inspiration. I have written this book to attempt to connect all these lessons I have learned in a way that inspires readers and helps them embrace what it takes to make their own *Millionaire Journey!*

ACKNOWLEDGMENTS

First, I want to thank all the mentors who have helped me reach financial freedom. They are enumerated in the book, so I will not spend more time on that here. I have never, at this point, had more than a brief handshake or email exchange, but I am so inspired by the efforts they have made to help others that I am choosing to do the same for the rest of my life.

Next I want to thank my parents. Both Roland (Ron) Green and Naomi Ruth Kirby, who taught me where money comes from: *work!* The single, most important value to wealth building is work ethic, and both my parents gave me examples of that in the way they lived their lives. Additionally, despite divorces, bankruptcy, and changes in custody through the years, I never had any doubt that they both loved me with all their hearts. Being secure in being loved offers a solid foundation that withstands the worst of storms that life may throw at us. The other thing that I need to thank them both for is the mistakes they made. I was able to learn much from the pain that they went through, and I have endeavored to avoid that pain by taking a different course of action, and that strategy has worked well for me and my family.

That brings me to the core of my being, my family. With all thanks to God, I am so blessed by the life that my wife, Karen, and our two boys, Michael and Tyler, and I have been privileged to live. We have seen God's blessing, provision, and protection in our lives so many times in so many ways. The faith he has given us in times of adversity and trials are only exceeded by His faithfulness to us. I am convinced that our Father in heaven wants to and will "work all things together for the good for those who love Him and are called according to His purpose."

Finally, I want to acknowledge my father-in-law, Tyler Jackson Moore. He modeled our heavenly Father's love better than any other man I know. Though he went to be with the Lord before this book was drafted, I am convinced that without his example for my beautiful wife, our boys, and me, our understanding of the goodness of the Father's heart would not have been solid enough to enable us to take the risks and walk in faith as we have. Ultimately, his example of unwavering faith in God's provision, protection, and goodness allowed us to make our *Millionaire Journey*.

INTRODUCTION

Get on Track

I Thought I Could, and I Did!

If I can do it, anybody can; and I have. I am a millionaire. I am not even fifty-five years old, and I am a millionaire. To some, that sounds unbelievably incredible. To others, it is mundane.

This book is written to the former. That is where I came from. I am the son of a broken family. My dad was married and divorced four times; my mom married three. My father filed bankruptcy, and we lost our house when I was eleven years old. He died a pauper in a Medicaid nursing home at age fifty-nine. I bounced from one home to another throughout my childhood.

When I became a young adult, I went to college. I was the first one of my family to do so, but I dropped out after two years. I languished in menial jobs for a couple more years, but then something changed. I got married to the most beautiful, intelligent, twenty-year-old Southern belle the world has ever seen. We thought we were going to be missionaries and save the world, but the reality of our first short-term mission trip showed us that was not the path for us. I needed a new plan, and I had no clue how to figure out what that should be. I eventually earned a bachelor's degree in history ten years after high school graduation, and three years later, at the age of thirty-one, I finished my MBA.

The point is, it took me thirteen years after high school to position myself for my career, and I am still a millionaire before fifty-five! Becoming a millionaire today is not rocket science. Anybody can do this. Yet I look around at our society, and people seem so hopeless in this regard. I want to be an ambassador of hope!

To that end I am going to share how I became a millionaire by fifty-five. The lessons I will share are very simple. In fact, I would say most of the things that I have learned about success really are simple strategies, applied with discipline over time. Focused intensity over time yields the results that we all long for in our lives, including Financial Freedom.

Your Journey to Financial Freedom

The premise of this book is simple. Wealth building is a journey. The journey takes place on a railroad. The railroad goes from the land of "Normal" to "Millionaire Mountain." The vehicle used on this railroad is your own personal life train. Your life train runs on the track of intentionality, and if you keep your locomotive on that track of intentionality, you will one day reach the land of "Financial Freedom" just the other side of Millionaire Mountain. The journey is long, uphill, and arduous. It is a journey that wanderers will never make; one has to be intentional.

This picture of our journey to financial freedom was inspired by a story we all knew as kids: "The Little Engine That Could." If you recall, the little engine's mantra was "I think I can I think I can. I think I can," as he labored and strained to make it up the mountain.

The track to becoming a millionaire is a reality, especially for those of us who live in the United States. Anyone can choose to drive his or her life train on the track and become a millionaire, but it is an uphill ride, all the way! One has to have the discipline and stamina for the long haul. In today's society, we lack people who "think they can." Hopelessness abounds. Society and politicians seem to feed that hopelessness and helplessness. It is a victim mentality that rules the land.

Derek Sivers in his book, *Secrets of the Millionaire Mind*, states it well. "It's time to decide. You can be a victim, *or* you can be rich, but you can't be both. Listen up! Every time, and I mean *every* time you blame, justify or complain you are *slitting your financial throat.*" Thinking like a victim is like slicing your own financial throat. Instead, we need to adopt the mantra of little engine that could: "I think I can. I think I can. I think I can."

If You Think You Can, I Will Show You How!

If you are ready to make the journey from the land of Normal, living paycheck to paycheck, juggling debtors, with no plan and no hope, to the land of financial freedom, I will show you the way. In this book, I will walk you through a real-world process, not a theory, that will take you from wherever you are in the land of Normal to the kind of life you dream of living—one where you are free to live, and give, as much as you desire without being burdened with care and concern of how you will pay for it! *Freedom* is out there, and I will show you how to get there.

Seven Steps to Journey from Normal to Financial Freedom

These tips, if followed, will guarantee you punch your ticket to the land of Financial Freedom. They are simple, but they are not easy. I will unpack each one in detail, but to end the suspense, here they are:

1. **Make up your mind to go**: Think for yourself. Don't be normal!
2. **Get to the train station**: Take only what you need. Leave the rest behind!
3. **Pick the right track**: Three-legged stool: passion, skills, and value in the marketplace.
4. **Pick your train:** Job Train, Career Train, or Entrepreneurial Express?

5. **Fuel the engine:** Invest continuously to keep the train moving.
6. **Look at the landscape:** Enjoy the ride, find new opportunities, and explore the world.
7. **Leave a legacy**: Impact the world by leading and giving.

Are you ready for the ride? If so, buckle up with me as we begin the journey. All aboard!

CHAPTER 1

Step 1: Make Up Your Mind to Go

*A*nother *Friday afternoon—thank God! You leave work and pull onto the freeway for another ninety-minute commute home. You wonder if you'll go out tonight. Your friends cannot seem to make up their minds about what they want to do. They're leaning toward clubbing, and you don't really want to do that. Sometimes you wonder if these guys will ever grow up. It's like college fraternity days are being relived, but you're ready for something more than hangover Saturdays, followed by football on Sunday, and then back to the grind on Monday.*

All of this introspection seems to be getting you nowhere. You're in debt up to your eyeballs from college loans. Your job is not that exciting, but it pays well enough to pay the bills—most months anyway. Just then, your phone rings. The gang is meeting at your favorite bar at eight o'clock. "Okay, I'll see you there," you reply. Like you said, where is all this introspection getting you anyway!

The land of Normal

I have to start off by quoting my financial mentor, Dave Ramsey: "Normal sucks!" As a regular listener to his online radio show, I have heard this statement from him countless times, and he is right! Our society has thrown off the conventional wisdom of our grandparents

1

to work hard, save up, and buy things we want. Now we are buying stuff that we don't need to impress people who we don't know, and we're doing it with money that we don't have. We have replaced wisdom with conventional stupidity in order to get what we want, when we want it, by utilizing debt and never considering the total costs of such behavior.

The average American is drowning in debt. Consider the following chart published by the Motley Fool. It shows the average balances on indebtedness by type of account in households that have that type of debt.

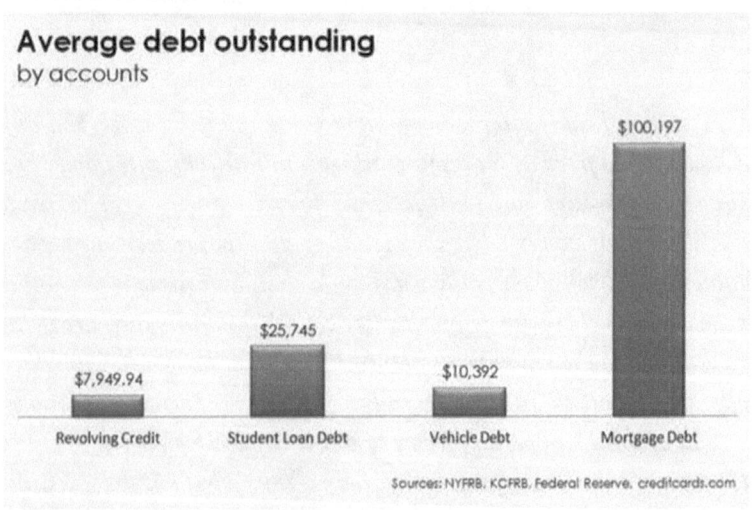

Couple this data with a 2015 study from the Government Accountability Office, which can be found on CNBC.com, showing only 48 percent of Americans aged fifty-five and over have any money saved for retirement. And those who do between the ages of fifty-five to sixty-four only have an average of $104,000, and those over sixty-five have only $148,000 saved. Estimated inflation-protected annuities would generate $310 in monthly income for the first group, and $649 monthly for the second—hardly the recipe for retiring with dignity!

If you want to be normal, there is nothing I can do to help you. If, however, you want to be weird and be a millionaire before age fifty-five, I can certainly offer you hope and a plan! Consider the following story and see if it does not give you some hope!

Even a "Loser" Can Be a Millionaire

Let me introduce you to Luke. Many would say Luke is a loser. He is eighteen years old and recently got his GED. He is working at a local furniture store, doing warehouse and delivery work, and he is making ten dollars per hour. Luke has gleaned one bit of wisdom in his eighteen years. He has decided he is going to live within his means and pay himself first by investing 15 percent of his salary in a nonmatching 401(k) plan at work, which is invested in an S&P index fund.

It is a good thing that Luke learned this one wise principle, because it is the only thing that keeps him from being the loser people think that he is. As Luke's life unfolds over the next thirty-seven years, he works at the same place, doing the same job, for the same pay. He never gets a promotion, and never gets a penny raise, but he keeps living within his means and invests $260 per month (15 percent of his $20,800 annual salary). Now, Luke is fifty-five years old. The index fund he put his retirement into averaged a 10 percent annual rate of return over the last thirty-seven years. Luke's contributions have totaled $113,582 over that time. He has decided he cannot keep lifting furniture for a living, and he begins to wonder whether or not he can afford to retire early.

He mentions this to his buddies at lunch one day, and the owner of the furniture store overhears him. "Luke," he says, "I own this place and cannot retire; you are dreaming if you think you can. You only make ten dollars per hour!"

"Maybe you are right," Luke says. "How much do you think someone needs to retire these days?"

"At least a million bucks," says the owner.

"Awesome," answers Luke, "here is my two weeks' notice!"

Luke, the "loser," had amassed $1,249,397. The furniture-store owner stands slack-jawed as Luke hands him his notice and walks away. Luke met with his financial advisor and mapped out a strategy to draw up to 6 percent, over $72,000 per year, and never touch the principal of his investments. He figured he would be just fine, and maybe he would write a book on his simple strategy to become a millionaire and add to his million!

Luke's Retirement Account

Age	Beginning Balance	Contributions	Growth	Ending Balance
18	0	3,120	312	3,432
19	3,432	3,120	655	7,207
20	7,207	3,120	1,033	11,360
21	11,360	3,120	1,448	15,928
22	15,928	3,120	1,905	20,953
23	20,953	3,120	2,407	26,480
24	26,480	3,120	2,960	32,560
25	32,560	3,120	3,568	39,248
26	39,248	3,120	4,237	46,605
27	46,605	3,120	4,972	54,697
28	54,697	3,120	5,782	63,599
29	63,599	3,120	6,672	73,391
30	73,391	3,120	7,651	84,162
31	84,162	3,120	8,728	96,010
32	96,010	3,120	9,913	109,043
33	109,043	3,120	11,216	123,379
34	123,379	3,120	12,650	139,149
35	139,149	3,120	14,227	156,496
36	156,496	3,120	15,962	175,578
37	175,578	3,120	17,870	196,568

38	196,568	3,120	19,969	219,657
39	219,657	3,120	22,278	245,054
40	245,054	3,120	24,817	272,992
41	272,992	3,120	27,611	303,723
42	303,723	3,120	30,684	337,527
43	337,527	3,120	34,065	374,712
44	374,712	3,120	37,783	415,615
45	415,615	3,120	41,874	460,609
46	460,609	3,120	46,373	510,101
47	510,101	3,120	51,322	564,543
48	564,543	3,120	56,766	624,430
49	624,430	3,120	62,755	690,305
50	690,305	3,120	69,342	762,767
51	762,767	3,120	76,589	842,476
52	842,476	3,120	84,560	930,156
53	930,156	3,120	93,328	1,026,603
54	1,026,603	3,120	102,972	1,132,696
55	1,132,696	3,120	113,582	1,249,397

You might say this is fantasy, and you would be right, but the math is valid. Making ten dollars per hour is certainly possible, saving 15 percent off the top is a decision one can make, and investing in an index fund within a retirement fund is easy. Finally, earning a 10 percent annual rate of return in an S&P index fund over thirty-seven years has been historically achievable. The reality is that if you are not a millionaire by fifty-five in the United States of America, it is probably because you have chosen (consciously or not) *not* to be one. That would make *you* the loser, not Luke!

The American dream is alive and well. According to an article in the *New York Post* on June 11, 2014, 44 percent of the world's millionaires live in the United States. According to the Spectrum Group as reported by CNBC in March 2015, there are approximately

10.1 million "high net-worth households." This group has over one million dollars in investable assets not including their primary residences. The same year, Statisticbrain.com reported just over 115,000 millionaire households in the United States. This means that approximately one in eleven people you pass on the street in the United States are millionaires. The first thought you might then have is, *Well aren't they the lucky ones?* The truth is that luck has very little to do with it!

Thomas Stanley, in his book *The Millionaire Next Door,* found that approximately 80 percent of millionaires in the United States are first-generation rich. They are self-made men and women who have become wealthy by working hard, living beneath their means, and consistently investing over the course of their lives. I am one of those people, and I can tell you with authority that I am nothing special! If I can do it, you can too, but you have to take the first step.

The first step is to *make up your mind to go*. You have to be willing to break away from what I call *the vortex of normal*. There is a gravitational pull toward normal in our society, and remember: normal sucks!

When you decide to make the journey to Millionaire Mountain and the land of Financial Freedom beyond that, you will see people coming out of the woodwork to tell you that you are crazy to think you can rise above normal, eradicate debt from your life, own your home outright, and have over a million dollars in investable assets. Your broke brother-in-law will tell you it is smart to put everything on your credit cards to get the points or the airline miles. Your dad will tell you that you will always have a car payment—or two. Your broker will tell you to keep your mortgage for the tax deduction and so you can invest more in the market and make money on the spread. There will be no end to the litany of reasons that you should not even try to take this journey. When you start to hear this feedback, I want you to *remember the crabs*.

When my first son, Michael, was ten years old, I took him away for a long weekend to spend some quality time and have the first talk about things he would go through in adolescence. He got to pick the location and activities, and he picked going to the beach and mostly fishing. We had a great time that weekend. The fishing was not very productive, but we caught a lot of crabs while trying to catch fish. The stupid crabs would not let go of our bait until they reached the surface, so we got our net, scooped them up, and put them in our cooler.

Lesson #1 from the Crabs: Don't Hold on to the Bait until It's Too Late!

Credit card companies are the most ingenious marketers on the planet. You may think that you are winning. You may think that because you are one of the 29 percent that are paying off their balances per month (per credit.com), and racking up airline miles, cash back, or other rewards. But in reality, people who use credit cards spend 12–18 percent more than those who spend cash according to Nerd Wallet.com.

Clinical psychologist and blogger for Psycholgy.com Art Markman, PhD, puts it this way," To stay within a budget using a credit card, you have to remember the prices for each of the items and then keep track of how those prices relate to your overall budget. If you have cash, then you can also limit the amount of cash that you carry as a way of limiting the amount you spend." If you think you are getting rich on your 1–2 percent cash back when you are spending 12–18 percent more, you are the crab holding on to the bait, my friend!

Lesson #2 from the Crabs: Beware the Other Crabs!

When Michael and I were having fun catching crabs, we noted an interesting phenomenon. When we would catch a crab and throw it in the cooler, one or two of the crabs would start to try to climb out of the cooler and escape. When they did, the other crabs would reach up with their claws, and pull them back down. Then one of the others might climb on top of the one pulled back, and try to escape, but once again, the group would reach up and pull that one back down into the morass of flailing crustaceans. In reality we started just leaving the lid open on the cooler because the crabs self-policed and kept each other from escaping.

You will find if you decide to make this journey, there will be many people around you who will dissuade you from taking the step from thinking to doing. Some of them will be very well-intentioned but ignorant. Others will operate from self-interest.

Consider a situation where you receive a $250,000 inheritance and ask your broker if you should use it to pay off your 4 percent, $250,000 mortgage or invest with him in good growth-stock mutual funds. It will be a rare individual who will advise you to pay off the debt rather than invest. Just know that in most cases, the conventional advice to invest the money will result in over $3,500 per year for your broker and his company, for the rest of your life. If your advisor works for your bank, paying off the mortgage would also cost the bank $10,000 the first year and probably over $100,000 for the life of the mortgage. Does that factor into their advice? Of course it does!

You need to be educated enough to make decisions based on what is better for you, not what is better for the other crabs. Certainly seek advice from professionals, but look for ones who will help you on your journey, not inhibit you from getting there!

So are you encouraged now? Are you ready to take the journey from the land of Normal to Millionaire Mountain and the land of Financial Freedom beyond or are you still worried that you do not have what it takes to get there? Well, let me tell you about a *force* that can propel you to success. Once you understand that this force is currently working *against* you if you are normal, but can be used *for* you to make you wealthy, you will hopefully be ready to make up your mind to go and move on to step 2 of *your* Millionaire Journey!

CHAPTER 2

Use the Force (Like Luke!)

The Power of Compound Interest

How did a loser like Luke end up a millionaire by fifty-five? The secret is in the power of compounding interest. This secret is what separates those who live paycheck to paycheck from those who reach Financial Freedom and leave a financial legacy that extends beyond their life-span. Financial guru Dave Ramsey uses an example to illustrate the power of compound interest. It is the story of two brothers named Ben and Arthur. I have slightly modified his illustration below to demonstrate the power of compound interest.

Ben is a self-starter and matured early. He started working while he was in college and decided he was going to save $2,000 per year. He invested that in an S&P index fund within a retirement account. He did this all throughout college, including grad school to get his master's and PhD, which he finished at the age of twenty-six. At that point, Ben decided to be a missionary and never contributed another penny to his retirement account from age twenty-seven to sixty-five. Over that period his investments earned a 10 percent annual rate of return. Ben only contributed $18,000 toward retirement in his entire life.

Arthur was the younger brother, and when he went off to college, he did not get a job. He, too, went to grad school for a master's and PhD and finished at the age of twenty-six beginning his career as a college professor. At this point, he decided to start saving for retirement and invested $2,000 per year in an S&P index fund earning a 10 percent annual rate of return from the time he was twenty-seven until retirement at age sixty-five. This means that Arthur contributed $78,000 over his life-span for retirement, or more than four times what his brother invested.

The amazing thing is that Ben actually amassed more wealth at retirement than did Arthur (See chart below).

Ben's Retirement Account					Arthur's Retirement Account				
Age	Beginning Balance	Investment	Growth	Ending Balance	Age	Beginning Balance	Investment	Growth	Ending Balance
18	0	2,000	200	2,200	18	0		0	0
19	2,200	2,000	420	4,620	19	0		0	0
20	4,620	2,000	662	7,282	20	0		0	0
21	7,282	2,000	928	10,210	21	0		0	0
22	10,210	2,000	1,221	13,431	22	0		0	0
23	13,431	2,000	1,543	16,974	23	0		0	0
24	16,974	2,000	1,897	20,872	24	0		0	0
25	20,872	2,000	2,287	25,159	25	0		0	0
26	25,159	2,000	2,716	29,875	26	0		0	0
27	29,875		2,987	32,862	27	0	2,000	200	2,200
28	32,862		3,286	36,149	28	2,200	2,000	420	4,620
29	36,149		3,615	39,763	29	4,620	2,000	662	7,282
30	39,763		3,976	43,740	30	7,282	2,000	928	10,210
31	43,740		4,374	48,114	31	10,210	2,000	1,221	13,431
32	48,114		4,811	52,925	32	13,431	2,000	1,543	16,974
33	52,925		5,293	58,218	33	16,974	2,000	1,897	20,872
34	58,218		5,822	64,039	34	20,872	2,000	2,287	25,159
35	64,039		6,404	70,443	35	25,159	2,000	2,716	29,875
36	70,443		7,044	77,488	36	29,875	2,000	3,187	35,062
37	77,488		7,749	85,236	37	35,062	2,000	3,706	40,769
38	85,236		8,524	93,760	38	40,769	2,000	4,277	47,045
39	93,760		9,376	103,136	39	47,045	2,000	4,905	53,950
40	103,136		10,314	113,450	40	53,950	2,000	5,595	61,545
41	113,450		11,345	124,795	41	61,545	2,000	6,354	69,899
42	124,795		12,479	137,274	42	69,899	2,000	7,190	79,089
43	137,274		13,727	151,002	43	79,089	2,000	8,109	89,198

44	151,002		15,100	166,102	44	89,198	2,000	9,120	100,318
45	166,102		16,610	182,712	45	100,318	2,000	10,232	112,550
46	182,712		18,271	200,983	46	112,550	2,000	11,455	126,005
47	200,983		20,098	221,081	47	126,005	2,000	12,800	140,805
48	221,081		22,108	243,189	48	140,805	2,000	14,281	157,086
49	243,189		24,319	267,508	49	157,086	2,000	15,909	174,995
50	267,508		26,751	294,259	50	174,995	2,000	17,699	194,694
51	294,259		29,426	323,685	51	194,694	2,000	19,669	216,364
52	323,685		32,369	356,054	52	216,364	2,000	21,836	240,200
53	356,054		35,605	391,659	53	240,200	2,000	24,220	266,420
54	391,659		39,166	430,825	54	266,420	2,000	26,842	295,262
55	430,825		43,083	473,908	55	295,262	2,000	29,726	326,988
56	473,908		47,391	521,298	56	326,988	2,000	32,899	361,887
57	521,298		52,130	573,428	57	361,887	2,000	36,389	400,276
58	573,428		57,343	630,771	58	400,276	2,000	40,228	442,503
59	630,771		63,077	693,848	59	442,503	2,000	44,450	488,953
60	693,848		69,385	763,233	60	488,953	2,000	49,095	540,049
61	763,233		76,323	839,556	61	540,049	2,000	54,205	596,254
62	839,556		83,956	923,512	62	596,254	2,000	59,825	658,079
63	923,512		92,351	1,015,863	63	658,079	2,000	66,008	726,087
64	1,015,863		101,586	1,117,449	64	726,087	2,000	72,809	800,896
65	1,117,449		111,745	1,229,194	65	800,896	2,000	80,290	883,185
Totals		18,000	1,211,194		Totals		78,000	805,185	

Compound interest requires time to produce results. The lesson from Ben and Arthur's example is start saving *now!* The sooner you start, the sooner the power of compound interest works for you to help you build wealth!

Rule of 72

One other piece of information that can help you understand the impact of compound interest is the *rule of 72*. That rule states that whatever interest or investment rate of return you achieve divided by 72 will give you the number of years it takes to double the value of your investment. In the Ben and Arthur example they both achieved a 10 percent rate of return, so their investments will double, on average, every 7.2 years:

Rule of 72 calculation for 10 percent rate of return: 72/10=7.2

To see this principle at work, look at Ben's chart and compare the balance at age 27 and age 34 and you see it goes from a little over $32,000 to a little over $64,000.

In our family we used the rule of 72 for a motivational tool with our younger son to get excited about investing. We started a "401-Dad" program at our house when my younger son, Tyler, was about nine years old. Every year around Thanksgiving, we would match what our boys saved. Tyler and I started an eBay business by buying at yard sales and estate sales and selling items online, splitting the profit fifty-fifty. This earned income allowed him to contribute to a Roth IRA each year. How did we motivate a nine-year-old to invest in a Roth IRA rather than spend it on video-gaming systems and toys? We taught him the rule of 72 and showed him how, if he could save $8,000 in a Roth IRA by age sixteen and leave it invested, he would likely have a million dollars at age sixty-five.

A Roth IRA invested in good growth-stock mutual funds will likely earn 10 percent annual return, so the fund will double every seven years or so:

Tyler's Retirement

Age	Roth Balance
16	$8,000
23	$16,000
30	$32,000
37	$64,000
44	$128,000
51	$256,000
58	$512,000
65	$1,024,000

Tyler was always good at math and a natural saver. He hit his $8,000 goal and has not taken any money from the account thus far. At nineteen, he has about $11,000 in the account and is well on his way to being a millionaire. The power of compound interest will likely turn his $8,000 into $1 million at retirement!

The Dark Side of Compound Interest—*Debt!*

Compound interest is obviously a powerful force. It is a force that can propel you to wealth or destine you to mediocrity or even poverty. It is a force that can be used for you or against you. It can set you free or put you in bondage. The reality is that you have the power to choose how this force will be used in your life. Will you invest and unleash the force to build wealth and leave a positive legacy, or will you choose to instead borrow money and spend your life in the bondage of debt paying interest to banks that could have gone to fund your retirement or your kids' college funds?

Car Debt

According to Experian, the average new car payment as I am writing this is $471.00 per month! The prevailing thinking is that every family will have at least one car payment, if not two! Let's look at what that mentality will cost you. Let's say that instead of paying a car payment you pay yourself $471 per month from age 30 to age 70:

Car Payment versus Retirement

Age	Beginning Balance	Contributions	Growth	Ending Balance
30	0	5,652	565	6,217
31	6,217	5,652	1,187	13,056
32	13,056	5,652	1,871	20,579
33	20,579	5,652	2,623	28,854
34	28,854	5,652	3,451	37,957
35	37,957	5,652	4,361	47,969
36	47,969	5,652	5,362	58,984

PATRICK M. GREEN, MBA

37	58,984	5,652	6,464	71,099
38	71,099	5,652	7,675	84,426
39	84,426	5,652	9,008	99,086
40	99,086	5,652	10,474	115,212
41	115,212	5,652	12,086	132,950
42	132,950	5,652	13,860	152,463
43	152,463	5,652	15,811	173,926
44	173,926	5,652	17,958	197,536
45	197,536	5,652	20,319	223,507
46	223,507	5,652	22,916	252,075
47	252,075	5,652	25,773	283,499
48	283,499	5,652	28,915	318,066
49	318,066	5,652	32,372	356,090
50	356,090	5,652	36,174	397,916
51	397,916	5,652	40,357	443,925
52	443,925	5,652	44,958	494,535
53	494,535	5,652	50,019	550,206
54	550,206	5,652	55,586	611,443
55	611,443	5,652	61,710	678,805
56	678,805	5,652	68,446	752,903
57	752,903	5,652	75,855	834,410
58	834,410	5,652	84,006	924,068
59	924,068	5,652	92,972	1,022,692
60	1,022,692	5,652	102,834	1,131,179
61	1,131,179	5,652	113,683	1,250,514
62	1,250,514	5,652	125,617	1,381,782
63	1,381,782	5,652	138,743	1,526,178
64	1,526,178	5,652	153,183	1,685,013
65	1,685,013	5,652	169,066	1,859,731
66	1,859,731	5,652	186,538	2,051,921

67	2,051,921	5,652	205,757	2,263,331
68	2,263,331	5,652	226,898	2,495,881
69	2,495,881	5,652	250,153	2,751,686
70	2,751,686	5,652	275,734	3,033,072

If you choose to always have one new car payment, it will cost you $3,000,000! Don't give in to the dark side of the force of compound interest. Use the force for good!

Mortgage Debt

There are few people who do not believe they will always have car loans, but fewer still believe they will ever pay off their mortgage. In fact, most people see mortgage debt as "good debt." Let's examine that a little closer. According to the Mortgage Bankers Association, the average mortgage in the United States is $294,900. Most people get a thirty-year mortgage and the prevailing thirty-year rate at the time of this writing is 4.125 percent. The cost of this "good debt" to the average American will be $219,624 in interest expense over the course of the loan. Is there an alternative? Is it realistic to save up and pay for a house? For most people, I think not. It is, however, possible to buy less house and pay it off over a shorter period of time, minimizing the burden of interest that has to be paid and allowing the opportunity to become completely debt-free.

Let's stick with the average mortgage to illustrate the difference between financing with a fifteen-year rather than a thirty-year. Average Joe decides to buy this average house at thirty-five years of age and gets a fifteen-year rather than a thirty-year mortgage. The first advantage he gets is that his interest rate drops from 4.125 percent to 3.5 percent. He does have a higher payment of $2,108.19 versus $1,429.23, but his interest expense will decrease from $294,900 to $84,574. That is a savings of $135,050. Now picture Joe fifteen years later. He is now fifty years old, owns his house, and put that

$135,050 in college funds for his two girls. What was so good about that mortgage debt?

Wait a minute. I know why I need that mortgage. It gives me a tax deduction! How many of your broke friends have told you that conventional *wisdom*?" Let us take a look at that idea.

In our thirty-year mortgage example, the first year's interest expense was $12,069. Let's say our mortgage holder makes $75,000 putting him in a 25 percent tax bracket. The $12,069 deduction will result in a tax savings of $3,017.32. So, if that makes sense to you, I will be happy to make you the same deal. You send me $12,069 and I will gladly send you $3,017.32. I love making people happy, especially when it makes me money, and so do the banks! If you don't like that idea you could always send the $12,069 to your favorite charity and still get you the same deduction.

So if you give in to the dark side of the force and keep your thirty-year mortgage, you just need to tell your kids to figure out how to pay for their college, and your charity will probably survive without your donation. After all, you need to stay in debt for another fifteen years and help support the profitability of your bank. They are a deserving institution, and we know how much they need money. Soon, your kids will be helping them as well. Student loans are another form of "good debt" that no one can live without! (That was sarcasm, by the way!)

Then one day as you are driving home, you hear this guy on the radio talking about erasing debt from your life. He is telling you that money matters and how to manage your money for the good of your family instead of just letting it slip through your fingers! A switch flips inside you. You've had it! You can't live in bondage anymore. You've determined you are leaving Normal. You're getting out of debt and starting your journey to financial freedom!

Your friends call you crazy! Your parents are afraid you've joined some kind of cult. After all, they've had car payments and credit cards their whole lives, and they're doing just fine. You go in to your bank to pay off a student loan; the banker congratulates you and tells you now qualify for a platinum credit card. You want to scream, but instead you just turn and leave without a word. You determine to go home, pack your things, and leave. You have made up your mind.

CHAPTER 3

Step 2: Get to the Train Station!

*O*nce you decide to make the journey, the next step is to get to the train station!

The land of Normal spreads out on a vast plain and it is teeming with people. Getting from place to place is easy as long as you move in the same direction and at the same pace as everyone else. Everyone moves around the land in a circular motion, always clockwise, until they reach their location where there will be a convenient exit ramp. People just go with the flow. They get up in the morning, hop on the highway, get off at their work or school exit, do their work, hop back on, and go home. Occasionally, they will stop on their way home to have some fun with dinner or a movie and then head back home. On weekends or holidays, they may hit the outer belt, get to the beach or mountains, and then return to the inner route to pick up where they left off. Round and round and round they go, day after day, year after year.

There are a few people who are different. Different is not welcome in Normal. These people are very evident, because instead of going around the circle like everyone else, they cut across the grain, rubbing people the wrong way along the way. People will yell at them, shove them, and try to drag them back into the flow, but they will not be dissuaded. Without fail, when someone asks these wayward offenders where they think they *are going, they always respond with things like, "I have to find a way out of this," "I have to get out of this rat race," "I can't go on living like this," "I feel like a rat in a wheel," yada yada yada.*

These people are all heading to the center of the land of Normal. In the center there is a hill. Everyone in Normal can see it from wherever they are. It is called Hope Hill, but the residents of Normal laugh at the name, saying Hope left Normal a long time ago! On the hill is an old train station that everyone says should have been condemned long ago, but somehow there are trains that still come and go every day. All the people in Normal can tell you about the people who struggled to Hope Hill to catch one of those trains attempting to reach the "fantasy land" of financial freedom, only to return to the land of Normal weeks, months, or years later, defeated and downtrodden. Those people were the more fortunate of the people who left. There were also many who did not return, but everyone knew what happened to them as well. They died of course. They had everything they needed in the land of Normal but chose to pursue folly and lost everything they had. If only they had listened to reason and settled in to the "good life" here in Normal! That's what all the "normal" people say.

The truth of the matter is that it is hard to leave Normal. There is a gravitational force that goes with the circular pattern of the rat race of Normal. It sucks you down and keeps you going round in the flow. From the top of Hope Hill, you can look down and see the mass of humanity, going with the flow to nowhere. It takes a tremendous amount of effort to break free from the gravitational pull of the rat wheel, and you will receive little hope from others. In fact, most will try to convince you that resistance is futile. Some will do it out of genuine concern, because they live in fear; others will do it because they do not want anyone to prove that their fatalist attitude is wrong.

Debt Is Dumb!

In the real world, that force pulling at you is debt. The writer of the Proverb was correct when he said, "The borrower is slave to the lender." The truth is that you are not free to do what you want to do if you are in debt. Let me give you an example from my youth, when I still lived in the land of Normal.

I grew up as a child of divorce, and both of my parents' households were lower-middle-class income families, so when I went off to a state college I was able to do so with federal grants and work-study programs due to my families' low incomes. I did not have to take out any debt. Unfortunately, I dropped out of college after two years. I was just immature and did not have clear direction in my life, so I bailed and moved in with my grandma for a while, trying to sort things out. I decided I wanted to serve others and concluded the best way to do that was to go into the ministry. I enrolled in a Christian college and talked my mom and stepdad into signing up for a school loan to pursue this dream. That pursuit lasted one semester. Due to some health issues with my father and his family, I struggled to complete my courses and decided to drop out.

The next year, at twenty-one, I decided to volunteer at a Christian boarding school for troubled teens as a live-in counselor and teacher assistant in the school. I received no pay, but the school committed to pay my student loan payments while I served with them. I thrived in this environment and was very fulfilled doing this work. Then one day, about ten months into this adventure, I had a message to leave the classroom and take a phone call. When I got on the phone, I was greeted with a very unpleasant individual from a collection agency who told me that my school loan was in default and that if I did not pay it in full that, they would garnishee my stepdad's wages. I was panicked. When I was eleven years old, my dad had had his wages garnished, and it was the final straw that caused him to file bankruptcy. I called one of my best friends (and the only one I knew that had a steady job!) and talked him into taking out a loan and allowing me to repay him monthly. He was able to do so, at usury rates of 25 percent! I immediately resigned my volunteer job to go back home in order to work and pay my friend back. I was one of the guys who tried to leave but was sucked back in to the land of Normal.

I am at a point, again, where I am able to do a lot of volunteer work, and I know many young people who have longed to go into Christian service, but the debt payments to service their school loans they accumulate getting their theological degree versus the market salary for these jobs does not have enough margin to meet other life goals. This leads these young people to go into further debt with car payments, credit cards, and so on. The result is many of them end up leaving their ministry pursuits in a few years in order to serve their other master—debt.

As hard as it is for young people just starting out to leave Normal, it is even harder for older people to do so. Why? Because the longer you are normal, the more indebtedness you amass, and the steep slope of indebtedness in the first decade of adulthood is breathtaking.

To further illustrate this point, consider these average credit card debt loads in 2012 by age group published on credit.org.

Age	Average Credit Card Debt
18–24	$3,000
25–34	$5,200
35–44	$6,200
45–54	$8,400
55–64	$8,200
Source:	credit.org (2012 data)

Then, there is student debt. This is particularly concerning because most of these are people trying to get out of the land of Normal.

Age	Average Balance per Borrower	# of Borrowers
Under 30	$20,412	15 Million
30–39	$29,364	10.9 Million
40–49	$27,828	6 Million

50–59	$23,820	4.7 Million
Over 60	$19,521	2.2 Million
Source:	nyfed.org (2012 Q4 data)	

College Debt is smart debt, many will say. Really? In 2012, according to the National Center for Education Statistics, 81 percent of high School students graduated. In 2011, the Bureau of Labor statistics reported that 68.3 percent of graduating high school students will attend college. According to the Department of Education 59 percent of College students will graduate with either an associate or bachelor's degree. So coupling all those statistics together, we can infer that if you graduate from college with an undergrad degree, you are in an elite percentage of the total population at 33 percent of high school students (.81*.683*.59). So, we now have over $1 trillion of taxpayer-backed student loan debt to help one-third of our young people? When that 33 percent graduate, how many really land a job that justifies the debt load they take on?

We will cover how to be one of the 33 percent without incurring debt in the next chapter, but reality in the land of Normal is that rarely occurs (about seven out of ten graduates used loans according to the Institute for College Access and Success's 2014 data), so even when one completes the task of graduating, she is sucked back into the vortex of Normal!

So if debt is the force that drags you back or keeps you in the land of Normal, the secret to escape is to never go in debt or to eliminate debt from your life to be able to journey to Millionaire Mountain and the land of Financial Freedom beyond it. In our allegory, you have to leave your debt to press through the masses and arrive at the train station. If you are a young high school graduate with no debt, this is much easier. If you are not, I would like to introduce you to the man with the plan to help you punch your ticket to Millionaire Mountain. He is one of my financial mentors, though I have only shaken his hand once in person. His name is Dave Ramsey.

Must-Haves Before Dave Ramsey's Baby Steps

Dave is famous for his step-by-step system to get out of debt and build wealth. They are his Seven Baby Steps, and we will be discussing those as we get you from the land of Normal to the land of Financial Freedom, but there are a couple of core principles that precede Dave's Baby Steps that are necessary to get you to the train station in the land of Normal.

An Old-Fashioned Map

In order to get to the train station, you need a map. A map? you say. Why would I use a map when I have a GPS and Google Maps? The problem is that using GPS and Google Maps is what normal people do, programmed by normal people to keep traffic flowing, and keep people from disrupting the flow. No, to get to the train station, you need to have a map that was created back when the train station was built around 1776. Back then, and for a couple centuries after, most people saw Hope Hill and believed that it was the route to get to Millionaire Mountain and Financial Freedom. People from the farthest corners of the land of Normal could see the hill as a beacon shining in hopelessness. Lately, however, the culture has shifted. Nobody normally takes time for the journey. Instead of working hard, saving, and achieving financial freedom, building character and self-esteem along the way, people have determined they are entitled to everything they want now and have given away their freedom to purchase the things they want with debt.

Normal people do not need a map; they simply plug their desired destination into their leased smartphones, and go on their way. Interestingly, they would never find the train station on their smartphone. The powers that rule the land of Normal have purposely left it off the map. Most citizens of Normal do not care that they have to go around Hope Hill to get to half of the things they are after. They follow the GPS, and the people in front of them, like so many sheep to the shearer and, eventually, the slaughter.

Must-Have #1: A Budget

The map to get to the train station is a plan to win. That plan is called a budget, and it is a must-have before we can start Dave Ramsey's "Baby Step" discussion. A budget gets people through the daily challenges and leaves gravity-laden debt behind. Without debt they will be able to move against the gravitational pull of the rat wheel and make their way, in a straight line, for Hope Hill and the train station. Budgeting takes discipline, and following the budget takes real work and, if you are married, a lot of communication. Life is changing, and in order to keep heading toward hope of something beyond Normal, you have to keep adjusting the plan to stay on course.

An Old-Fashioned Video Game

Back when I was a young adult, there was a very popular arcade game called Frogger. In the game you are a frog, and you are trying to get from point A to point B across a three-lane highway and a raging river. The people who were really good at the game found the patterns in the number of cars and speed of cars that would come at them, and they would plan their route accordingly. That is what we do when we budget. Based on the patterns and rhythm of life, we chart our courses, looking at the money we expect to receive, and we plan to pay the bills we know will be due before we receive more. If there is anything left over, we apply it to other life goals like vacations or retirement. Dave Ramsey often describes a budget this way on his radio show: "We give every dollar an assignment, on paper, on purpose, before the month begins."

In the game of Frogger, no matter how good you were, there were surprises you could not anticipate. You would know the pattern and start to cross the three lanes of traffic when, right in the place there should have been a gap for you to get across the second lane, the programmers would stick a snake! It was totally ridiculous because no snake travels forty-five miles an hour between trucks! This one did, and you would have to choose; do I get killed by the snake or get run off the road?

Must-Have #2—Insurance

Life will throw the unexpected at you as you begin to budget. There are snakes everywhere, and that leads us to the other must-have prior to starting Dave Ramsey's Baby Steps one through three, and that is Insurance. There are certain things in life for which almost no one can afford to budget. For these things it is better to **transfer risk**, by paying small amounts periodically to someone else who assumes all the risk.

Insurance to Never Be Without

Health—According to CNBC, Medical bills are the leading cause of bankruptcy, and in March 2013 a Huffington Post article quoted a Harvard study that attributed 62 percent of bankruptcies in America to medical expenses. In my childhood, two surgeries for me and two more for my father were the final straws that broke my family's financial back and led to my father filing bankruptcy. I have spent over thirty years as a healthcare administrator, and I can tell you firsthand that the expense associated with healthcare cannot be sustained by the vast majority of people. This is an insurance you cannot live without. In addition, most plans in our current era will require very high deductibles ($5K–$10K annually) so there will also need to be monthly money allocated in your budget to cover that in addition to insurance premiums to keep the medical expense snake from getting you.

Long-Term Disability—This insurance will replace a percentage of your income (usually 60–70 percent) should you become disabled after an "elimination period" (usually three to six months). One very important note about this type of insurance: make sure you pay these premiums with after-tax dollars. If you do, the benefits are not subject to federal income tax. If you buy them with pretax dollars, the benefits will be taxed!

Auto (if you own a car)—If you own a junker, you might consider just getting liability coverage, but if your car would be difficult financially for you to replace without debt, then full coverage would be in order.

Home Owner's or Renter's—Under either scenario, theft, fire, weather, liability can be protected against for very reasonable rates.

Personal Liability Umbrella (if you have significant assets)—We live in a litigious society, and if you have more than a few hundred thousand in assets you may be targeted for compensation beyond your auto or homeowner liability limits. For a couple hundred dollars a year, you can have an additional $1 million in coverage. It is money well spent.

Identity Theft Protection—ID theft is rampant. I have personally been identified in two breeches of which I am aware. The hassle that can come with straightening out the chaos resulting from someone stealing your identity can be overwhelming. There are companies that will take on the responsibility for that for less than $200 per year.

Term Life (if you have people who depend upon your income)—Everyone is going to die. The human race has a 100 percent mortality rate. The saddest stories I hear are the ones where an otherwise responsible spouse or parent dies without insurance, leaving his or her family to deal with financial calamity on top of emotional grief. Get term insurance in place for ten to twelve times one's income so that your family will not have to worry about making ends meet. They can invest the insurance funds to create replacement income for that of the deceased.

Dave Ramsey's Baby Steps One through Three

In order to be able to journey to Millionaire Mountain, you have to be debt-free and prepared for the journey, or you will wind up being dragged back to Normal by your debtors or turning around at a station down the line and returning because you did not have what it takes to complete the long trip. As I told you, there is a man with what I believe to be the best plan in the universe to ready you for this journey, and his name is Dave Ramsey. I could probably come up with something that takes Dave's principles that he has laid out so well in his book, *The Total Money Makeover,* and repackage them and "make them my own," but I believe in giving credit where credit is due, and pointing people to the place they can go to achieve their goals and dreams. Dave's company, Ramsey Solutions, has such great tools and infrastructure to support people in this journey, which I have personally used to succeed; it would be irresponsible of me *not* to tell you about them!

If you find yourself in the land of Normal, but have decided to catch the train from Hope Hill to Millionaire Mountain, once you have a budget and proper insurance coverages in place Dave Ramsey's first three Baby Steps will get you there:

Step One: Save a $1,000 "Baby" Emergency Fund

If you are a young college student with no family, low income, and low expenses, you might drop this to $500, but all the rest of us need $1,000 to help us not use a credit card for the little "snakes" that creep into our path while heading to the station. If you already have $1,000, or when you get it you are ready to move on to step two. If you have more than $1,000 in cash savings, you too may move on to step two, and I will tell you what to do with the extra cash when we get there. You will *only* have $1,000 to keep the wolf from the door, so get intense on your budgeting—no eating out, no movies, no vacation and no Starbucks! You should be *very* concerned with only $1,000 between you and life! Let that motivate you to get through these first three baby steps as quickly as possible!

Step Two: Pay Off Your Debt using the Debt Snowball

What is the debt snowball? First, you must be current on your debts, making the minimum monthly payments. List your debts smallest to largest (regardless of interest rates) and pay them off by paying all your minimum payments, attacking the smallest one with every extra dollar you can squeeze out of a scorched-earth budget. If you have bad debts where the lender is willing to settle in full, then set them to the side until you determine the lowest amount they might accept. Then add them back into the appropriate place in the snowball at that lower balance.

If you have savings over the $1,000, use it at this step on the smallest debts. If you do not, squeeze your budget as tightly as possible, throw every dollar you wring out of it monthly at the smallest debt, and work your way through the list. As you pay off the smallest debt, the minimum payment will be freed up to throw at the next smallest debt. As the snowball rolls over, it picks up more snow (or dough!) from the paid-off debts' minimum payments so that the amount you are attacking the next debt with gets bigger and bigger. The momentum you feel as each debt falls and the amount of money you free up gets bigger and bigger motivates you to keep going, adding intensity to your budgeting, selling everything in your attic, and making you willing to get second and third jobs because you now have hope and a plan!

What do you do if you do a budget, cut everything you can, and there is still too much month left at the end of your money? This is where a lot of people find themselves and why there is such a pervasive sense of hopelessness. The best way I know to illustrate this is with a word picture. Once upon a time, lumberjacks transported fallen trees via rivers. They floated the trees downriver from a location where they chopped them down to a place where they could sell them, transport them, or mill them into products for sale. Unfortunately, sometimes in that process the trees got hung up on curves in the river and create a logjam. Lumberjacks went out in the dangerous waters with poles and pushed the trees free, but sometimes the logjam was just too massive, and the only way they could break up the logjam was to throw dynamite in the middle of the floating logs and blow it up. It was an option of last resort as it destroyed good timber.

If one finds him- or herself in a financial logjam, he or she may need to take drastic action and blow something up. That person should eliminate debt by selling the cars, boats, motorcycles, and four-wheelers to eliminate the monthly payments. Forgo any entertainment that costs money such as vacations and eating out. He or she may need to work overtime and extra jobs like a maniac!

It is also important to prioritize first things first. During the housing crisis of 2008–2012, I heard of so many people who allowed their houses to be foreclosed on yet stayed current on their credit cards! If you do not have money for everything, first take care of food, then shelter, transportation, and basic clothing. Everything else can wait! These are the real necessities. Do not let some bully of a credit card collector deter you from those priorities.

Step Three: Save a Fully Funded Emergency Fund (Three to Six Months of Household Expenses)

As soon as you finish your debt snowball, while you are still in attack mode, let the momentum of the debt snowball now roll toward establishing a three-to-six-month emergency fund. This is a buffer that will protect you from the worst things life can throw at you like job loss, disability, divorce, and death of a loved one. Really, this is another form of insurance for things that insurance does not cover. If you get to the train station without this, you will not be prevented from getting on the train, but you are most likely going to be one of the passengers who turns around down the line, returns to Normal, and proves to others that they should not aspire to be anything other than what they are.

Many people have heartburn about keeping three to six months' worth of cash in a simple savings account or money market because they think that much money should be earning more money. The reality is that one's emergency fund should be thought of as insurance, not an investment. Insurance is something you have to protect your other assets. That is why you have an emergency fund in cash. If you invest that money, say in stock, and that investment goes in half like we saw in 2008, your emergency fund just went in half as well. In addition, you will not want to pull that money out for an emergency at that point because you will realize the loss. So instead, you will be tempted to go back in to debt to cover the emergency and wait for the investment to regain its previous value. That defeats the whole purpose of establishing the emergency fund to begin with. Leave this fund in a savings account or money market that cannot lose its value and repeat after me, "It is insurance, not an investment."

Cash is King

Baby steps one through three are all about getting you to a cash position in your life. This is completely countercultural. Why is this important for your financial success? There are three reasons:

1. It gives you control of your number-one wealth-building tool: your income! The normal reality for most people is they do not budget because their money is all spoken for before the month begins in the form of monthly payments on things purchased using debt. House, cars, school loans, credit cards, and home equity loan payments leave a lot of people with more month than money. Until one gets out of this mindset of "if I can make the payments, I can afford it," he or she will never get out of the land of Normal.
2. It saves you thousands, or even hundreds of thousands on interest expense. As we saw in the difference between fifteen-year and thirty-year mortgages, when you eliminate interest

your family benefits instead of the bank! People just do not stop and count the cost. If they did, they would never choose to live their life in debt!

3. *You spend less* when you spend cash versus plastic. Study after study has shown that people's spending increases when they use plastic versus cash. A 2007 research study at Carnegie Mellon University demonstrated under functional MRI scans that spending cash activates pain centers in the brain, while according to research coauthor George Lowenstein, "Credit cards effectively anesthetize the pain of paying." This is why credit cards are happy to give you airline miles or cash back. They know people will spend more, which make retailers happy, and therefore retailers will continue to pay the fees to have their brand of credit card available for you to use to make more purchases. If you think you are coming out ahead of these corporations that spend billions, you are deceiving yourself!

Can You Really Afford it?

When you are doing a budget, you ask yourself this question before any new purchase, but if you think like a Normal person, it still may not set you free. A Normal person thinks in terms of how much down and how much a month when they look at a potential purchase. Here is the typical scenario:

My car keeps breaking down, so I need a new car that is dependable. I can afford a new car, because they have a promo for zero down, three-year lease at $400/month. I spent $1,200 this month on car repairs, so it would be smarter to put that money into a new car.

In reality, at the end of that lease you will be upside down on a car that you have paid over $14,400, so you will have to pay the difference or roll over to a new lease on a new vehicle and perpetuate the cycle over the rest of your life. Depreciation on new cars will always cost more than maintaining a used vehicle.

This same "normal" logic is used to justify toys, vacations, vacation homes, rental property, and so on. Our society has a broken risk meter, and it has led us to be constantly teetering on the edge of bankruptcy. One unfortunate job loss, injury, divorce, illness, or what-have-you will take people down who use this logic. There is however an alternative thought process that will cause you to live in a way that will get you to Financial Freedom. "If I can't pay cash for it, I can't afford it." It is an old-fashioned concept, but it works!

CHAPTER 4

Step 3: Pick a track

You arrive at the train station on Hope Hill, prepared for the journey. You look around at an amazing sight. You are in the hub of a labyrinth of tunnels, tracks, and elevated tracks. There are platforms with people waiting everywhere you turn, with stairs and escalators and halls extending as far as you can see in every direction. You see a crowd gathered around a pillar in the center of the station, and you make your way toward the strange obelisk. As you approach, you see that the people gathered are of all sorts. You observe young and old, well dressed and vagrants, of all races, and, from their attire, apparently many different religions and cultures. Some of them are moving frantically from one of the four sides of the pillar to the other and then the other, while others seemed to be standing transfixed, and yet others are lost and dismayed. You see a man dressed in conductor attire, and you walk up to him and ask him for help. He informs you that this is the station map that you may use to find the right track to take you on your journey.

"I am looking for the track to Millionaire Mountain," you say. "Can you tell me which track goes there?"

"Why certainly," he answers. "All of these tracks could eventually lead to Millionaire Mountain, but you have to find the right track for you."

"I don't understand," you reply. "What do you mean, the right track for me?"

"If you have arrived here, it is because you understand there is something more out there than Normal. Deep inside, you want to be more than you can be in Normal and do more than you can do in Normal. This place was designed to help you find the right track, for you, to make the journey that only you can make," the conductor answers.

"Do you mean that everyone who comes here has his or her own track?" you inquire.

"Oh no!" the conductor answers. *"You will share the track you take all along your journey with others who are trying to reach the land of Financial Freedom, but you will have many stops along the way, each with the opportunity to go in many different directions, and as you select from those, you will create your own journey that you alone will be able to call yours. Others may share large portions of the journey with you, while some others will be strangers only passing on a platform."*

The Right Track for You

The first element of picking the right track is to determine what you will do to earn an income. This decision can paralyze people, leaving them stuck at the platform for years. Some people will tell you to follow your passions; others will tell you to follow the money. My advice is to follow both!

Dan Miller, author of *48 Days to the Work You Love* and *Wisdom Meets Passion*, has an illustration that explains this more fully. He describes finding meaningful work as having three components. First, you have to find something you are **passionate** about. Second, you must have **strong talents** in the arena you choose. Last, but not least, you have to have a **model to create income**. Where these three must-haves overlap is the sweet spot for work that matters. That is, fulfilling, purposeful, impactful work that will provide for you, your family, and your future.

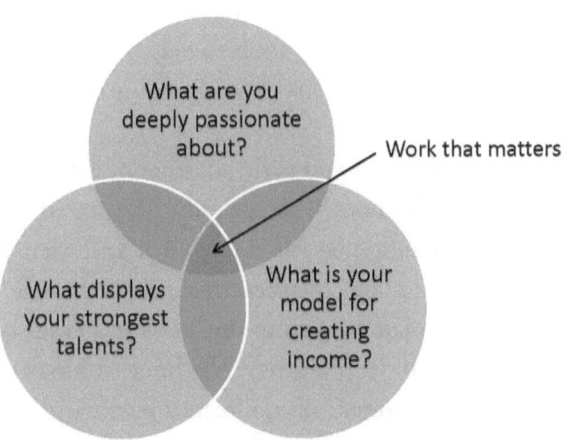

Dan describes this as a three-legged stool, and he says that if you only have two legs, the stool will eventually fall over. For instance, I have a passion for music, and I have a great business acumen, but I have very little musical talent. Pat Green is a great country music artist, but Patrick Green would "fall off his stool" if he was on the stage of the Grand Ole Opry. Likewise, many artistically talented individuals lack the passion to carry out the work necessary to make a living, and yet others have the skills and the passion but leave their success in the hands of fate rather than creating and following through on an economic model that will cause them to succeed in the business of doing their art.

Though this is an important decision, many people are not successful, because they are afraid of making a mistake. Rather than do something that could be wrong, they do nothing. They are the proverbial deer in the headlights. They are standing in the middle of the track, staring at the train, trying to decide whether to go this way or that. All the while, life is passing them by.

Take some time and do some introspection using Dan Miller's books above or others such as *Quitter* or *Start* by Jon Acuff, *The Purpose-Driven Life* by Rick Warren, or *Strengths Finder* by Tom Rath to help you clarify your sweet spot. Use personality-survey tools such as a Meyers-Briggs personality profile, StrengthsFinder 2.0 profile, and or DISC profile tools to help you. These books and survey tools have helped millions of people figure out what they were made to do with their lives.

Go back to childhood and early adulthood, if you have passed that stage, and think about what you always wanted to do when you grew up. Figure out what you are good at and what you would do even if no one paid you, then research people who do that for a living, and create a plan for you to do the same. Find someone to mentor or coach you in your journey. The Internet has made experts so accessible. Take advantage of it. Create a plan!

The Figure-It-Out-in-College Fallacy

Many would tell you the thing to do is to get an education. They would point out that you don't know what you do not know. They would suggest that college is a place you can get answers by exploring the world through the experiences of others. Heading off to college is obviously the right thing to do next, right?

For those who would offer this advice, I would suggest that though they mean well, this approach has not proven to work out for most. First, according to an article posted in *US News & World Report* online on November 10, 2015, 19 percent of high school students will not graduate. For these students, college is not the answer. Couple that with the fact that only 65.9 percent of high school graduates will enroll in college this year according to a *New York Times* (nytimes.com), April 2014 article, and that means that college only applies to approximately 53 percent of high school students. Add to that the fact that only 59 percent of college students graduate within six years of enrolling (US Department of Education study, 2013), and the math says that only 31.5 percent of high school students actually graduate from college. Are they the only ones who can leave Normal behind? No! According to Investopedia.com, 20 percent of millionaires are *not* college graduates! Does college give you an advantage? Clearly. Is it for everyone? Certainly not!

Does not going to college doom others to a life of mediocrity? I say emphatically *no!* The majority of college students are not figuring it out! They are starting out farther behind than when they graduated from high school.

Education is extremely important, but sending eighteen-year-olds off to college without parental involvement and direction and expecting them to figure out what they will do with the rest of their lives is *not* working out. Let's start with the 41 percent who do not graduate. According to the College Board, the average price tag for tuition, room, board, and fees for a year of private college is $32,405. State college averages are $9,410 for in-state students and $23,893 for out-of-state students in the 2015–2016 school year. Even if all 41 percent of the dropouts did so after one year, that is a huge price tag to pay if you do not end up getting a degree. If everyone paid for it with cash, it would be bad enough, but the reality is that 71 percent of all students who graduate have school loans, and we have no reason to believe it less of a percentage for dropouts (Institute of College Access and Success, 2012).

Moreover, according to a 2014 CareerBuilder survey, 51 percent of the graduates from that year who were employed reported that they were not in a job that required a college degree. Meanwhile, they are buried in school debt. According to the *Wall Street Journal*, the average college borrower graduated in 2015 with over $35,000 in debt.

So there we have it. That is the "normal way." Send your kids off to college to find themselves, and the result is that 41 percent of them drop out in debt, and 30 percent (51 percent of 59 percent) of them end up $35,000 in debt and in jobs that they could have had four years earlier. That leaves 29 percent who graduated and got a "real" job.

Results We Are Looking For?

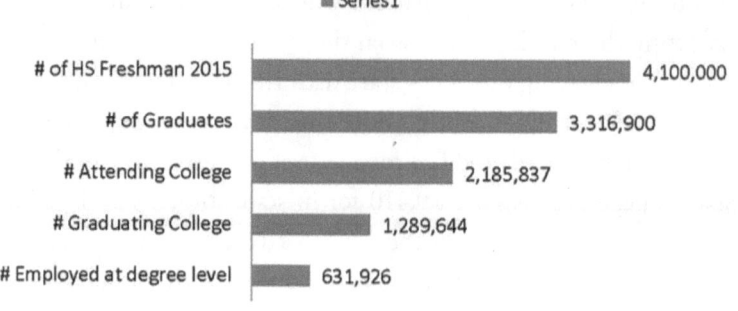

The graph above summarizes how we are doing as a society on educating our young people. According to the National Center for Education Statistics, the freshman high school class of 2015–2016 school year was approximately 4.1 million students. Applying the percentages from the research above, here is the future we can expect for those students. Of them, 3.3 million will graduate from high school, 2.2 million will attend college, 1.3 million will graduate, but only 632,000 will find employment that required the degree they worked so hard to get. That means we are creating a system where 15 percent of students win. I think we should and *can* do better than that! I suggest that there is a better way.

Parental Oversight

First, parents, stay engaged. Go through the exercises above with your kids to help them find out where their passions, talents, and abilities to win in the marketplace overlap. If they have not figured it out by the time they are going to college and you have the money saved for them to go without taking on debt, college can be a great time and place for them to experience some things to figure it out, but stay involved. Help them select majors that will translate to incomes that will meet their life goals. Make sure that their education includes internships or side jobs in the fields they are considering, so they can test the theory of what they think they will like and succeed in before they are locked in to a track to nowhere! Encourage them to change majors while they are still in their core coursework, so they can move on to something better but still finish in four years. Require them to start working with the college career-placement office by their second semester to secure the best internships out there and make the connections that will lead to them having multiple offers when they graduate.

College Is Not for Everyone

If we start with finding the overlap between people's passions, talents, and methods of monetizing themselves in the marketplace, we will often find that a traditional four-year degree will not benefit many people. A degree in computer science, for instance, is almost useless today. What is taught in the university setting is a decade behind what is used in the marketplace. Certifications on the most current software platforms will take people much farther in that world than a four-year degree.

If someone has a passion for real estate, there is no need to invest tens of thousands of dollars in a college education. That person can easily study for the real estate exam and get a license without a day of college. After succeeding and saving, he or she can take the acquired knowledge, invest in real estate, and become very wealthy, all without a college degree.

Some people want to work with their hands, and trade schools may be the vehicle to a successful career. Yet others may learn on the job through apprenticeships. All of these avenues are viable, depending on which track you are choosing in life.

College has gained this mystique in our society as though it is a rite of passage into adulthood. Parents push their children into college whether or not they or the students can afford it, and they believe they are doing the best thing for their children. Sadly, today's student debt crisis shows us that those good intentions are leading many into a prison of debt.

Do Education Debt-Free

Whether college is right for the student or not, some sort of education is likely to be necessary to set out on a successful career track. Until one gets that education, he or she cannot really experience the career she thinks she wants, and, therefore, cannot be certain that it will be the right fit for him or her. With that being the reality, whatever education one needs, find a way to get it without incurring debt.

Debt is an anchor. It will keep you from moving forward if you know the direction you want to go, but probably more importantly, it will keep you from moving on if you realize you made a mistake and need to move in a different direction. Your choices are limited by the weight of the debt and the monthly payments they inflict upon you. What is so sad is it is all unnecessary. It is completely feasible to get an education, including a four-year college degree or even a graduate degree, without going into debt.

According to the College Board, the average four-year in-state tuition and fees for the 2015–2016 school year was $9,410. If a student waits tables, delivers pizza, or does any part-time job twenty hours per week, fifty weeks per year and makes $10 per hour, they can cover the cost of tuition and fees. If they work full-time in the summer and breaks, they could even make enough to live on campus. They could cut expenses even further by attending a community college for the first two years where the average tuition and fees drops to $3,435.

If a student wants to go to a private college or out-of-state college, the cost will be exponentially higher. I have heard so many parents justify tens of thousands in debt to get their child to the "right school." This usually has to do with a belief that certain schools will give you an advantage when looking for a job. With certain exceptions for ultra-elite schools, and then for only certain career fields (Harvard for law, Wharton for business, etc.), there is no evidence that such is the case. In his book, *View from the Top*, D. Michael Lindsay, PhD, wrote about research he conducted on five hundred fifty elite leaders, including two hundred fifty top CEOs of Fortune 500 companies. He found that over two-thirds of them graduated from nonelite schools. If the majority of elite leaders are from nonelite schools, how much more likely that leaders of average to good companies could succeed without the "elite school" education and the price tag that comes with it?

The other thing I have heard used to justify more expensive schools is that it is the student's "dream school." This usually boils down to the aesthetics, sports teams, or status. All of these factors are fine if one can afford them. None of them make sense if the parents or student have to go into debt. Many college dropouts and graduates alike would testify that debt has turned their "dream school" into a living nightmare.

Debt-Free Graduate School

Another fallacy is that you might be able to go to undergraduate school debt-free, but you cannot hope to accomplish the same for graduate school. The figures for the cost of postsecondary education are not as readily available as undergraduate, and therefore the research takes longer and the data is more dated, but as of 2010, *US News & World Report* found the average postgraduate degree program at an in-state public institution costs $30,000 including housing costs. Allowing for inflation, let us round that up to $36,000, or $18,000 per year for a two-year program. The same math we used for undergraduate covered $10,000 per year working part-time. If one is working in his or her field of study, there is almost always a tuition-reimbursement program available to cover the other $8,000 per year. If not, one may need to work full-time for a year or two, save, and go back to graduate school when one has the money. An alternative may be online graduate degrees, which are typically less expensive and can even be done over a longer period of time around a full-time job.

Student Loan Debt Is the *Dumbest* Debt

The ultimate irony is that using federally backed student loans is the absolute stupidest debt instruments to take on. Why? They are not eligible for bankruptcy, nor are they negotiable. Why would a bank ever negotiate when the American taxpayers are on the hook for the loan, plus interest, plus any penalties and fees? Why would the federal government allow a bankruptcy when they would have to pay all of the above? It is, therefore, worse than any other debt. There is only three ways to get rid of student loans. Pay them off, die, or become disabled. Do *not* believe the lie that school debt is smart debt.

What about the Adult Students?

This subject is near and dear to me. I was in this category. I graduated from high school, went to college for two years, and dropped out. I resumed my college career four years after getting married. I got my associate's, bachelor's, and master's degrees as an adult student. That was many years ago, but I can encourage you in this part of the story because I have lived it.

My wife and I were barely making ends meet while both she and I went back for our degrees. There were twists and turns along the way. I changed majors twice. We found a great deal of assistance out there in the form of grants and scholarships. I got tuition reimbursement from my jobs and took side jobs, and we both persevered, getting our degrees in careers we knew we loved, because we experienced them by working in them as we pursued our degrees.

The United States is still the land of opportunity, with great programs to help those who need it and income potential for those who can do it on their own. If one looks for the opportunities, instead of floating down the path of least resistance, one can absolutely get the education one needs without being swamped by a tidal wave of debt.

The Bottom Line

The bottom line is that education will be necessary for almost anything you set out to do, but if you select the right level of education in the right setting to allow you to pay as you go and acquire the skills you really need, you will afford yourself the freedom to pursue your dreams no matter where the winds of opportunity may take you. It will take forethought and planning, but it is completely doable in modern society. You just have to be intentional.

Ain't Nothing to It but to Do It!

Once you have your plan, strike out on the journey! Don't let fear paralyze you any longer. Start doing something. Take steps toward finding or creating your dream job. If you pick a wrong track, it will still be all right! Since you have chosen to take the journey without debt, there will be a station down the line where you can stop and get your bearings and redirect if necessary. Doing something is better than nothing. Failing forward is the way most successful people have made their journeys to Financial Freedom. Very few of them picked the right track from day one. There will likely be many stops and starts, twists and turns. Don't get discouraged by them. Embrace them, learn from them, and refine your plan.

Lessons I Learned from My Sons

I am blessed to have two great young men whom God has given me the privilege to call my sons—Michael, who is currently twenty-three, and Tyler, who is nineteen. They are both excellent scholars, have worked hard in their academic careers, and have, therefore, a world of options in front of them.

Tyler is attending the only college he really cared to get into, and he plans to be an attorney. We already have a plan to get his undergraduate degree without debt, and we will continue to craft a plan as his education unfolds toward getting his graduate degree in law. He has obtained scholarships that will pay for his tuition and fees, leaving us to only cover his living expenses for his undergrad degree. He has decided to major in business as an undergrad because it will leave open more options than a prelaw or political science major in case he finds other passions than the law, knowing the skills will translate well to manage or own a law firm in the future.

We already know the most likely universities he would attend for law school, the costs to attend, and savings goals he will have to meet to pay as he goes. He is confident this is the direction he wants to go, because he actually worked in a law firm after his junior and senior years of high school. He will continue to look for similar opportunities through internships or part-time work or both while he completes his undergraduate degree. I am confident he will be one of the 15 percent that get it right!

Michael graduated from high school in 2012, graduated with his bachelors of science in finance in December 2014 and his master's in finance in December 2015. He is working as a tax specialist in a financial planning firm, and he has already passed the prestigious certified financial planner examination. After a few more months working in his field, he will be able to add "CFP" (certified financial planner) to the other letters behind his name at the ripe old age of twenty-three!

How did my boys set themselves up to launch so well? Here are the lessons I put forth as the keys to their and other students' successes in making the educational system work for them:

Work in the Real World

Michael started a lawn-care business at the age of thirteen. His maternal grandfather, "Pawpaw," taught him how to do it well, to very exacting standards, and he took that excellence to the market of our neighborhood and made great money. Later he took jobs in retail and at a golf course and proved his work ethic over and over again.

Tyler started differently. After making thousands buying at yard sales and selling on eBay, he decided he needed to experience working for others, and he took a job cleaning pools in the Atlanta summer heat. He left that to take the aforementioned position at a law firm, where he really excelled and confirmed that he wanted to work toward a law degree.

Michael, despite having a full-ride scholarship for his undergrad, decided to work in college to get more work experience and make himself attractive to prospective employers upon graduation. He did internships at two financial planning firms for a total of three semesters, and he worked one tax season as a tax preparer for a well-known national firm. He also tried his hand at real estate, getting his broker's license and impressing regional leaders for another national firm in that arena. As Michael approached his undergrad graduation, he had many options from which to choose, but he also had learned a lot about himself. He knew where his strengths lay and where they intersected with his passions, and he could pick from employers that gave him the best opportunity to leverage those in the marketplace.

Build a Resume Early

College is very competitive because easy access to school loans has greatly increased the number of students who start college. In order to stand out, it is important to know that colleges are looking for students they believe have what it takes to finish. They are looking for people who not only excel in academics but also have leadership skills, contribute to their communities, and have some balance in their lives. High school students who recognize this and are intentional about doing those things and capturing them on a resume shine above those who do not. Michael constructed a resume in his junior year and revised it regularly until he received a full-ride academic scholarship to a school he knew could take him where he wanted to go. Tyler did the same, which helped him land scholarships and gain acceptance to his dream school.

Leadership Opportunities Are All Around and Most Are Free or Affordable

Both Michael and Tyler excelled in this arena. Though different in temperament and style, both have become leaders. Both attended a very affordable program in Atlanta called "21st Century Leaders" that allowed them to interact with leaders from Fortune 500 companies and top educators to learn and practice leadership skills. School clubs were another vehicle that Michael utilized. He ran for and held officer titles in more than one club in high school. If you do not find one where you think you can lead, all you have to do is start one! Most high schools will start any club a student devises as long as there is a faculty member willing to act as an advisor. Church and civic organizations welcome students to step up and contribute. Tyler has been a leader in our church's student program, helping lead middle-school small groups for two years. This was an important part of the resume he built for his college application and scholarships.

Show that You Are Well Rounded

Students will not thrive on academics alone. Both of my boys were able to letter in a sport—Michael in track, Tyler in tennis. If that is not a possibility, students can point to recreation league sports, art classes, film projects, photography, musical accomplishments, writing, or blogging, and so on, and highlight those on your resume and applications.

Give Academics and Standardized Tests Your Very Best Effort

Three factors are still the most important to college admissions offices:

- **Grade Point Average:** This is still probably the single most important statistic looked at by colleges. Different schools have different thresholds, but almost all of them are very concerned with this measure.

- **Academic Rigor:** Back in my day, this was pretty simple. You were on the college prep track, or you were not, but today there are far more choices. Advanced placement classes are the norm for students planning to attend college, and now schools have added actual dual enrollment where high school students attend college classes on college campuses as part of their high school education. These latter two developments are not only raising the bar for college admission offices but also providing an excellent opportunity for students to obtain college credits at a very low price point. Michael was able to start college with enough credits to be a college sophomore and was smart enough to work with advisors to use his four-year full-ride scholarship to obtain all but one semester of credits necessary to get his master's in finance.
- **SAT or ACT Scores:** Over the last couple of decades, as the rigor options have increased, these tests have become more relied upon to help assess where students really are compared to other students. Both Michael and Tyler took their first PSAT test in seventh grade and their first SAT test as sophomores in high school. We paid for both young men to take focused tutoring, which improved their tests scores over several attempts to get them to the point where they achieved scholarships that paid for most of their college. It was probably the best investment in time, effort, and money that they, and we as parents, made in their futures.

Apply, Apply, Apply for Scholarships and Grants

As I said, both boys benefited greatly from scholarships. My wife and I have done well financially, so they were not eligible for needs-based scholarships or grants. Nevertheless, they were able to get scholarships. Both of them applied for many, many more scholarships than they received. The secret to getting scholarships is to apply. Furthermore, don't stop at undergrad. When you get to college, make friends with people in your financial aid office and in the college of your major. Michael not only leveraged his four-year full-ride to get some of his master's degree funded but also went to his college and obtained a teacher assistant position and additional scholarship money to completely cover his master's degree program. If you will be intentional and thorough, there is a lot of money out there. If you are in financial need, there are a lot more out there than for what my two boys were eligible to apply. Go after that free money! One word of warning about this: student loans are often disguised in a way that can make them look like grants or scholarships! Read the fine print!

Work in the Field You Want to Enter

The main reason Michael chose the college he attended was the full-ride scholarship, but the reason he even applied to that college was because he saw what that college did to provide internships to business honors students. They not only suggested internships but also required it and guaranteed they would help the student secure one. As I stated before, Michael took full advantage, and his work experience allowed him to secure his first "real job" in a firm he knew matched not only his financial desires but also his business philosophy and level of service he believed clients deserve. He would not have known that without over two years of real-world experience working in his field.

I really cannot take credit for Michael and Tyler's successes, but I can tell you they made the decisions they made after long discussions with their mom and me. We stayed engaged in their lives because we know that sending eighteen-year-olds off to college without involvement is like giving a sixteen-year-old a new car without ever teaching them how to drive. They *will* wreck their lives!

CHAPTER 5

Step 4: Pick a Train

You have determined what track you are taking, and after consulting the map, you have headed for your platform to pick up your train and start your journey. When you reach your platform, you find that there are three trains waiting. The first looks like it chugged right out the nineteenth century. There is a steam locomotive with a passenger car, a few box cars including a tender car to house the coal that fuels it, and a little red caboose. Next there is a locomotive from the mid-twentieth century, pulling a much longer train with several passenger cars, and dozens of box cars. Finally, there is a twenty-first-century electric bullet train, silver and sleek with the appearance of a jet airplane without wings. There is nothing but passenger cars for this train. Maximized speed and comfort are epitomized in this piece of technology.

You look around, and to your surprise the same conductor you spoke with in the main station is now here on the platform with you. "Excuse me," you say as you walk up to the man in the black uniform. "Can you tell me which one of these trains I should take to set off on my journey? I know this is the right track, but I am not sure which one is the right train?"

"Why, that choice is completely up to you. You may take whichever train you choose for this journey," the black-clad man answered.

"How do I choose between them?" you inquire.

"The first train is the job train," the conductor responded. You can set out immediately if you select this train. It will require less preparation, and overall there are more of these trains available if you change tracks on down the line, so your waits will be shorter, and therefore you can keep your forward momentum fairly easily, but it is by far the slowest of your options and will therefore likely take you longer to reach Millionaire Mountain: probably thirty to forty years.

"The second train is the career train. You will have to do a little more planning and preparation to embark on this train, and if you decide to change tracks on down the line, you may have to wait a while to catch the next one heading in the new direction, because they are much rarer than the job trains. The good news is that career trains could get you to Millionaire Mountain and Financial Freedom more quickly, probably in the twenty-to-thirty-year range. It also could take you a lot further than the job train, possibly even to the Multimillionaire Mountain range deep in the land of Financial Freedom.

"The third train you see here is the Entrepreneurial Express. It is far faster and can travel much further than either of the other trains, but let me show you something." The conductor walks over to the sleek, silver bullet train. "Come here and touch this train," he implores.

So you walk over and reach out your hand, but when you think you should have touched the rocket-shaped mode of transportation, the train shimmers, and you feel nothing but air. You try again, with the same result. You look up at the conductor who is now wearing a wry smile.

"It is a hologram," he explains. It is a model, but in order to take this train on your journey, you must first build it."

"Build it? How would I ever build such a machine!" you exclaim.

"It is not easy," the conductor explains, "but others have done it. They have written instructions for people who come behind them that want to try to do it on their own at the start of their journey. Other travelers will start out on one of the other trains and work their way up to building their own entrepreneurial express by studying about how to build one as they make their journey, going places and doing things along the way they believe will help them one day build their own *entrepreneurial express. The choice is yours. It is your journey, and you can pick any of these three options that fit you."*

Get a Job!

This is option #1. Remember our story about Luke who worked delivering furniture for $10 per hour and retired a millionaire? It really can be done, and there are those who enjoy working as landscapers, receptionists, or retail clerks, and never want the stress of building a career or building their own business. The reality is that people can do that and make saving and investing a priority, and they can still reach retirement as millionaires, but these people are very rare. The reason is that our culture and economy is built on a marketing engine that convinces people to have it all now and worry about paying it back later. Of course that dark side of compound interest keeps banks rich and people poor. It usually takes people back to the land of Normal and it makes it even harder to make the decision to leave Normal again.

If what you want to do is be a forest ranger, turn a wrench in a garage, paint houses, that is absolutely awesome! If you want to hold doors in New York City, deliver mail in Topeka, Kansas, or wrangle cattle in Wyoming for the rest of your life, you are free to do so. If you want to work nights at a hotel front desk so you can pier fish all day because that is what gives you joy, then do that. You are one of the fortunate few who live in a society where you can do those things and still retire wealthy. In his book *Retire Inspired*, author Chris Hogan points out that if you make $34,000 per year, which translates to a $16 or $17 per hour job, you are in the top 1 percent of income earners in the world. That's right; almost all of you reading this book are "one-percenters!" If any of you tell me you cannot save $100 per month, you have some explaining to do to the other 99 percent of the world population! Set up your life so that the $100 per month is the priority, and you will eventually achieve financial freedom.

I would like to make one comment about those of you who

choose this old-fashioned train option. As you travel down the track you choose, you may see opportunities to take the skills you have learned and alter your courses by switching tracks and or switching trains. You may decide you know how to fix cars better than the guy that owns the garage you work in or that you could tutor children that aspire to ride and rope on the junior rodeo circuit. Maybe you could set up a clinic for all the rich tourists who come to your pier to fish, who end up catching nothing but sunburn. Opportunities are all around us if we look for them. Many people choose to get a *job* because they assume that building a career or their own business is beyond their reach, when in reality if we work at things we are passionate about, there is almost always an opportunity to help others with the same passions and be well rewarded in the process.

Develop Your Career

The main difference in this approach versus people who select the *job* train is that they set off with the knowledge they want to advance in their work. There are many different examples of this. One may choose a profession and look to prepare academically while getting practical experience. A physician, attorney, accountant, nurse, or teacher would all be examples of professions that integrate academics and practical experience.

Another such example is tradesmen who start as apprentices in their fields, but over time advance to positions as journeymen and finally masters of their craft. Similarly, many in the military build careers, rising through the ranks. Likewise, state and federal government workers in various areas of service advance through different levels and pay grades as they grow in experience and in span of leadership control. Last, but not least, corporations offer people the opportunity to rise through creating value within their companies whether by salesmanship, leadership, or service to their fellow workers in support roles.

In our capitalist society, the opportunity to advance is literally everywhere you turn. That creates hope and forward momentum.

Why then is there so much hopelessness in America today? What has caused the despair that we see all around us? What keeps drawing people back to the "vortex of Normal"?

I believe the answer is indebtedness. The culture of have it now and pay me later has created a situation where young people are acquiring the lifestyles of their parents in their twenties and early thirties and spend the rest of their lives trying to pay for it. The problem is that they have lost the number-one tool for building wealth—their incomes! The money comes into their checking account and goes out to their creditors leaving nothing to show for it. They have no margin left to build wealth or enable flexibility. If an opportunity comes along to advance their career, they are not in a position to relocate, or be without an income for sixty days to start their own companies, or to change their educational tracks after two years, because they are under the bondage of indebtedness. If instead we could teach them to go slow, pay as you go, and create a pad of money to help them navigate the twists and turns that the journey throws at them, they will be able to turn on a dime and pursue their dreams wherever they may take them.

Do Your Own Thing

Working for yourself, to many, is the ultimate expression of financial freedom. You can set your own hours, integrate with your lifestyle, and keep all the profits your work generates rather than making some owner rich. Instead of "working for the man," you are the man—or woman, as the case may be. Picture yourself on that bullet train to Millionaire Mountain! It looks like an easy ride, doesn't it?

Starting your own business and home ownership are pillars of what most see as the American dream. According to the 2010 US Census, there were 27.9 million businesses with less than five hundred employees versus 18,500 with five hundred or more. A Forbes study in 2013 found 28 million such small businesses. The Small Business Administration website in 2016 uses the same 28 million statistic and goes further to assert that those businesses account for fifty-five million jobs in the United States.

Interestingly, according to Forbes, 22 million of the 28 million small businesses are sole proprietorships, with no employees. Solopreneurs, as many have called them, come in all shapes and sizes. They may be professionals like CPAs or attorneys, tradesmen like plumbers or carpenters, salespeople working for multiple distribution chains, or retired career people who are now acting as consultants or coaches, leveraging the knowledge skills and networking relationships they have acquired through the years.

The Internet has revolutionized the business landscape enabling success of the smallest businesses. The solopreneur can access services that used to be housed only in large corporations. Legal, marketing, accounting, and other professional services can be obtained on a per job basis. Masses can be reached for free utilizing social media platforms, blogs, and podcasts to build tribes of followers, making Madison Avenue marketing firms almost obsolete. Personal computing and smartphones enable working from anywhere, and enable one to reach his or her customers anywhere they are.

On the downside, all this technology has enabled competition like never before, from everywhere in the world. This drives down prices and makes work you can provide a commodity that can be farmed out to the lowest bidder anywhere in the world. This greatly increases risk associated with starting a business. Greater competition leads to greater risk of failure. The exact percentage of small business failures is a hotly debated topic. There are many variables, like how long of a horizon you set and what constitutes a "failure." Further, the reality that serial entrepreneurs that move from one business to another, displaced workers who start a business while looking for another job, and retirees who work a few extra years and then fully retire cloud the picture. Regardless, it is fairly certain that at least half of all small businesses fail within ten years.

Not everyone is willing to risk their family's livelihood on a coin flip. Even fewer are in a position to do so if they have tens of thousands in school loans and consumer debt. Unless we change the cultural norm of selling our future flexibility for today's lifestyle, our society will see less and less of these important job engines created. Further, if we do see people take the risk, but use indebtedness to fund that risky venture it will lead to more failures, less hope, and the belief that the little guy can't get ahead. If you are betting your future on a coin flip, at least own the coin!

Which Is the Right Train for You?

Let us first acknowledge that people can leave Normal at very different times in their lives. This may help determine which train you will select. If you have spent thirty years in Normal, you may have acquired a lot of knowledge to enable you to more quickly hop on the Career Train or Entrepreneurial Express than someone fresh out of high school. That is not to say that a young person absolutely should settle for a job. Take, for instance, a high school senior who is passionate about tennis, with skills and abilities that enabled him or her to be ranked nationally as a junior tennis player. Would he or she be able to start his or her own junior tennis academy out of a set of neighborhood tennis courts? It is quite possible. In fact, it might be easier for that person to catch the Entrepreneurial Express because he or she does not have to worry about feeding a family as he or she take the risk of being his or her own boss and garnering clients.

Maybe someone decides to leave Normal after thirty years, but he or she hates what he or she has done for a living during that time. For that person, leaving might mean taking a job train to provide for his or her family while that person gains a new skill set for which he or she has more passion and later can turn into lucrative career opportunities.

Whatever situation people are in when they catch their trains, there is a way out of Normal. In fact, I believe there are multiple tracks and trains that can get each person from Normal to the land of Financial Freedom. Keep in mind: you are not locked in for the long haul. There will be stations and stops along the way where you can change trains or tracks or both. In truth, the only mistake you can make that cannot be corrected later is the decision to not make the journey.

The most important thing is to keep the goal in sight and move toward it. Feel free to stop and get your bearings. Check in with others who are on the journey and learn from their experiences to avoid the traps and pitfalls that can reroute you back to the land of Normal. If the fog rolls in and you can't see the mountain, if your track takes you through a dense forest that prevents you from seeing the goal for which you are aiming, keep moving forward on the track you were on when you last saw the mountain in front of you. You will eventually reach your goal if you just keep your train moving forward. Whichever train you choose, and whichever track it is running on, you can get there from here if you just remember you can!

CHAPTER 6

Step 5: Fuel the Engine

You have picked your train, and you climb aboard and head to a passenger car. You sit down and wait. As far as you can tell, you are all alone on the train. In fact, the platform outside is empty as well. After a couple of hours, you wonder what you are doing here. You begin to think you have been duped and that this has all been for nothing. You start to think about leaving and heading back to the home you left in Normal when, outside on the platform, you once again see the black-garbed conductor, staring alternatively toward the train and then toward a gold pocket watch in his hand.

You open the window and call out to your guide. "Excuse me, when does this train leave the station?" you inquire.

"Why, that is entirely up to you," the conductor replies rather matter-of-factly.

"Oh, I did not know that!" you reply emphatically. "I am ready to go now then."

"Great. Let's get to it then." the man in black replies, and you see him step through the passenger car doorway and appear in the aisle heading toward you. When he reaches you, he keeps moving and calls out, "Don't just sit there—follow me."

And so you jump up and start working your way into the aisle to find the conductor is already moving on to the next car. You hurry to catch up with him as you make your way through two more cars and *find yourself trying to keep up with the conductor as he climbs a ladder and scrambles across a car full of coal, then down a ladder into the old steam engine of the job train you have selected to ride.*

"Here, put these overalls on so you can get to work," the conductor says as he hands you some very dirty, well-worn gray overalls, obviously stained by black soot.

"Get to work?" you ask. "Doing what?"

"Why, fueling your train, of course," he answers. "You cannot get to Millionaire Mountain unless you fuel the train, causing it to move down the track. This train works on coal, but it not just any old coal. It is investing coal. If you work hard, almost every day, and feed your train's engine with investing coal, the power will build upon itself making the travel easier. If, however, you get distracted and forget, or lazy and choose not to fuel the train engine consistently, the train will slow down, stall, and even roll backward back toward Normal.

Keep in mind that in order to leave the land of Normal, you've already unloaded debt from your life and your ticket was stamped only after you'd set aside an emergency fund of three to six months of expenses. The very next thing you need to do out of your income is invest. For people of faith, there are two stages of investment.

Stage one is to invest in the lives of others through tithes, offerings, and charitable contributions. Many believe that this giving is to benefit others, and surely that is one of the effects. Providing for local churches, synagogues, and charities to serve their communities and missionaries to reach the world with truth and love is certainly an important outcome of this giving, but I believe that giving works within the heart of the giver as well. Generous people are attractive people. They are well liked and trusted. People want to do business with them. People want to help them, and therefore they tend to attract even more money than the miserly can save. The very nature of generosity would never allow one to give more so they can receive more, yet in reality that is almost always the outcome. Therefore, to give first will almost always cause people to come out ahead of those who do not give.

If you are not a person of faith, you may choose to forgo this step, but I would argue that you will be missing out on the one thing that brings more joy than anything else you can do with money: *give it away!* If you don't believe me, give it a try. Leave that struggling, single-mom waitress a hundred-dollar tip. Buy Christmas for the family who lost everything in a house fire. Give your old car away to the drug-addiction program that is helping addicts turn their lives around so that one of them can drive twenty miles to the new job he just managed to land. I know you will not regret it.

If you are not at a point where you believe you can give of your *treasure* off the top, then I challenge you to instead give of your *time* and your *talents*. When I was a teenager, my stepfather did not practice tithing, which bothered my mother greatly. She decided that if she could not give a tithe of the family income, she would at least do it with her time. She served in various roles within her church and community and had a tremendous positive impact, not only in her community but also on the heart of her husband. At the end of my stepfather's life, before he lost a battle with cancer, he was as much of a giver as my mom.

Stage two is to pay yourself before you spend on lifestyle. The only way to assure you consistently have the fuel for your journey to Millionaire Mountain is to prioritize it by paying yourself before you spend on lifestyle. This is a theory made popular by David Bach in his book *The Automatic Millionaire*. He advocates setting up automatic deductions from payroll to 401(k) investment accounts or automatic bank drafts to IRA accounts so you never miss the money, a similar theory to what the IRS uses to take our tax payments from us in a way that does not cause us to revolt! We do not miss what we do not have. This is a good theory and can work well in practice, but it is not foolproof. Why? Because unlike taxes, we still have access to the money, and many who do not put the other elements of a financial plan together end up stealing from their investments to weather job losses, fund business start-ups, pay for kid's college, or to pay off consumer debts or school loans. This often results in being hit with as much as 50 percent in taxes and penalties for the right to access their money! Those hits will scramble a nest egg beyond repair in a hurry!

Remember: investing is done once you are out of debt and have an emergency fund. Other items you want to acquire must be cash flowed or saved up for rather than tapping into what you have put away in investments. If you invest and then steal from it, you will cause your engine to bog down and stall. Slow and steady wins the investing race. Never tap into your 401(k) or IRA unless you are doing so to avoid bankruptcy or foreclosure. The cost is too steep, not only of the money withdrawn today, but also with the money that money would have earned had it not been taken out of the investments. It is the "stupid tax" that keeps on taking for the rest of one's life!

Wisdom for Wealth Building from "Ramsey Solutions"

Both Dave Ramsey, in his book *The Total Money Makeover*, and Ramsey Solutions team member Chris Hogan in his book *Retire Inspired* lay out a simple, succinct plan for investing in Dave's Baby Steps Four, Five, and Six. The first thing to remember is that before you start this step, you have to have completed the first three Baby Steps. This means you are completely debt-free except for your house mortgage, and you have a big pile of cash accessible in a safe savings or money market account for emergencies. Then, and only then, should you move on to Baby Steps Four, Five, and Six. One thing that is different about these steps is you may do all three at the same time if you have enough margin in your budget. If you do not, then you still need to do them in this order prioritizing first Four, then Five, and then Six.

Baby Step Four

Invest the first 15 percent of your income for retirement utilizing tax-favored retirement accounts and invest in a series of good growth-stock mutual funds.

This single step will allow you to retire wealthy. Remember our example of Luke the loser, who retired a millionaire? Based on historical returns in the stock market, the math worked for him, and it will work for anyone. No one can guarantee returns in the future, but our best indicator is to look at history and do our best to learn from its lessons. Our work life will be approximately forty years on average. Pick any forty-year historical period and look at what the stock market has returned, and you will see this has been a sound strategy in the past. So let's break down this step and look at its components.

Tax-Favored Retirement Accounts

These accounts fall into two categories:

1. **After-tax contributions with no taxes on growth:**
    a. Roth IRA (limit $5,500/year under fifty years old, $6,500/year for fifty and over)
    b. Roth 401(k) (if your employer offers it)
    c. Roth 403(b) (if your nonprofit employer offers it)

2. **Tax deductible or pretax contributions where growth is taxed upon distribution:**
    a. Traditional IRA
    b. Traditional 401(k)
    c. Traditional 403(b) (like 401(k) for nonprofit companies)
    d. SEP IRA (if your employer offers it, or if you are self-employed)

When investing, most people will benefit more from the first type of accounts, as most of the money you end up with from investing will be from growth, not contributions, and most people will have lower earnings in retirement, putting them in a lower tax bracket at the point they start withdrawing the funds. The longer the horizon, the surer you are that after-tax contributions will be right for you. If you are going to access the funds within five years, or even ten, you might want to sit down with a great advisor who is a CPA or coordinates his advice with a CPA to analyze your particular situation. For the purpose of this illustration, we are going to assume the investor has twenty years or more until retirement.

The Power of the Match

Bob is thirty-five and has dug himself out of $45,000 of debt in the last two years while saving up his emergency fund. He makes $70,000 per year as an internal auditor at a hospital and is ready to start his retirement investing. His company only offers a traditional 403(b) plan but matches 50 percent of what he invests up to 6 percent of earnings. How should Bob invest his $10,500 annually (15 percent) for retirement?

The first rule of retirement investing is take advantage of the match. At Bob's hospital, this represents and instant 50 percent gain on his investment. The only time you would not do this is if you do not plan to be with the company long enough to be vested in the matching funds. This is typically a one- or two-year time frame. So for Bob this means that $4,200 ($350/month) would be invested in his 403(b) and instantly become $6,800 due to the employer match.

This leaves Bob with 9 percent or $6,300 per year to invest. Since Bob has a long horizon until retirement he would want to next put money above the match into an after-tax vehicle that would prevent the growth from being taxed. Since his employer does not offer a Roth 403(b) option, that means he would want to invest next in a Roth IRA up to the annual limit of $5,500 ($458.33/month). That leaves $800 to invest, which would mean he should go back to his 403(b) and fund it another $66.67 per month to his monthly contribution, bringing his monthly 403(b) contribution to $416.67.

Tax-Favored Accounts Are Not Investments!

Many people are confused about this point. If you ask them what they have their money invested in, they will say, "My 401(k)," or, "An IRA," not realizing that these are not investments! Let's take a minute to bring clarity to this important point. Let us define the specific tax-favored retirement account options above:

IRA: An IRA is an individual retirement account. Whether Roth (after tax) or traditional (tax deductible), it is not an investment, but rather a coat of armor that protects your investments from taxes.

401(k)s or 403(b)s: The names come from actual sections of the Internal Revenue Service's tax code. For instance, you can read about 401(k) regulations in section 401, subsection k. They act like an IRA, shielding your chosen investments from being taxed, but instead of them being individual accounts, they are accounts an employer sets up for its employees. Those called 401(k)s are set up by for-profit companies, whereas 403(b)s are set up by nonprofit companies.

SEP IRAs: These are Simplified Employee Pension Plans; IRAs set up by employers as well, but typically used by small employers, especially sole proprietorships. Again, investments placed in these accounts are protected from taxes by IRS regulations.

Entire books are written to explain these various options for retirement savings. There are rules around each of these options: limits of contributions, income limits for eligibility, and loopholes to get around the income limits. From my own personal experience, my recommendation is to get advice from an investment professional you can trust. They will be able to tell you the best vehicles for you and your family. I will cover how you might find an investment professional you can trust if you do not have one later.

All of these options are just vehicles to shelter investment income from taxes, not investments themselves. So what should you invest in within these retirement vehicles?

Investment Options
Cash Savings, CDs, or Money Markets: This is the most commonly thought of thing in which to place our wealth. *Money!* If you want to buy something, this is what you need. If you do nothing with it, you will have it when you need it, right?

This reminds me of an episode of the original, Rod Serling 1960s TV series, *Twilight Zone*. In the episode the main character decides he is going to put himself in cryotherapy for a few hundred years while waiting for the power of compound interest in his savings account with $10,000 or so, to make him rich! When he awakes from his deep sleep, he is indeed a multimillionaire! He is ecstatic that his plan has worked, or so he thinks. His illusions come crashing down when he stops by a grocery store to pick up a few things, and his tab is a few hundred thousand dollars!

Compound interest is a powerful force, but we must remember that that same force works against wealth in the form of *inflation*. Inflation is the rate at which prices increase. If our investments do not earn more than inflation, we will fall behind in our wealth building. In that scenario, inflation will overtake us and drag us down if we live long enough.

Leaving your money in cash under a mattress, or in CDs, savings accounts, or money markets will all leave you with returns lower than inflation. These are fixed investments that are safe. They will not go down in value as other investments might. Other than the mattress, they are typically insured by the federal government so you can get your money, even if your bank goes out of business.

Bonds and Bond Mutual Funds: These investments put you on the other side of the debt equation. You are the one loaning your money to an entity who pays you interest. These investments usually outpace inflation but carry less risk than stocks, also known as equities, because a company is obligated to pay its debts but is not obligated to provide a return on investment to its common stockholders. Bonds may be purchased for all manners of entities such as public companies, private companies, municipal governments, hospitals, and so on. Though there is a lower risk than equities, any of these entities can default on their debt obligations and leave the bond holder empty-handed, so they are not risk-free.

Bonds may be grouped together into bond funds and purchased by groups of investors who mutually fund these bond purchases. This provides for diversification across multiple bonds, so that if any one entity defaults, it does not completely destroy the value of the investment to any individual participating in the bond mutual fund.

Stocks and Stock Mutual Funds: These investments allow you to own a piece of the company you are investing in. The piece of the company you own is called a *share*, and it represents a percentage of equity in the company. This type of investment is available for public or private companies. The return on investment depends upon how the company performs. If they make more profit, their company becomes worth more, so the individual shares of the company are worth more. If the company goes bankrupt, a share of ownership goes to zero. Therefore, any individual stock represents a high risk.

Like bonds, public company stocks may be grouped together into *stock funds* and purchased by groups of investors who mutually fund these stock purchases. This provides for diversification across multiple companies, so that of any one entity defaults, it does not completely destroy the value of the investment to any individual participating in the *stock mutual fund*.

Index Funds: These are stock funds that attempt to mirror various indexes such as the Dow Jones Industrial Average, or Standard & Poor's 500. Let's use an S&P index fund as an example. Standard & Poor's rate the largest 500 companies on the New York Stock Exchange. Performance of these companies' individual stocks, in aggregate, is considered the best reflection of the US stock market as a whole. It is the benchmark that all other stocks, and indeed many other investments are measured against. If one is buying shares in this type of mutual fund, the fund managers are committing to you to buy stocks in each of the S&P companies in proper proportion to keep the returns equal to that index.

Exchange-Traded Funds: These type of funds are very similar to index funds above, but whereas mutual funds are only traded at the end of a trading day, ETFs can be bought and sold during the day, much like individual stocks. They also typically trigger fewer taxable events and are therefore usually, but not always, more tax efficient than mutual funds. To fully understand the differences between index funds and ETFs, meet with a financial advisor you trust and ask him or her to teach you.

Real Estate Investment Trusts (REITs): Real estate is the most commonly understood investment type because home ownership is such a big part of the American dream. Investment real estate is difficult to embark on, because it takes significant up-front capital. Many people, therefore, choose to borrow money to invest in real estate. This is a very risky approach, leading to many more failures than successes. There is now an alternative for investors to invest in real estate with very small amounts of capital through REITs. Similar to mutual funds, REITs sell shares to investors and use the money to purchase real estate. Real estate is then managed as rental property, or flipped for a profit, and the profit from these activities is shared with the shareholders of the trust.

Annuities: These are actually insurance products with investments inside of them. They can be either fixed (with a fixed rate of return) or variable (with a variable rate of return). The returns are usually greater than money market funds, but less than index funds, especially when comparatively high fees and commissions are netted against the returns.

This is not an exhaustive list of investment options, but it does cover the most common options available to be invested in tax-favored retirement accounts. With all of these options, what should any individual choose?

Investment Considerations

Cash flow needed for lifestyle desired: This is the starting point to figure out what your investment strategy should be. What do you want your retirement to look like? Are you willing to cut back your lifestyle in order to retire earlier, or do you need to work longer to build your nest egg to allow you to travel the world, or buy a beach house? Once you decide what you want in retirement, you can look at what you have saved, and compare that to what you might need to generate the cash you need to fund that desired lifestyle.

Risk tolerance and return: The next big factor is to consider what level of risk you are willing to take in order to generate what expected level of returns on your retirement nest egg. If you have $3 million at age sixty-five and want to maintain a $100,000 per year lifestyle you might be fine if you die by age ninety-five. On the other hand, if you have $2 million and want the same lifestyle, you need to die by eighty-five, or you need to earn something on the money in your retirement account.

There are some software tools that can help you do this analysis. I recommend two of them. First, to do a quick look at what you need to be shooting for I recommend the RIQ, or Retire Inspired Quotient, tool at chrishogan360.com. Then for a very in-depth analysis, I suggest the "Monte Carlo simulation" tool that uses an algorithm to help assess your likelihood of success of reaching your retirement goals. This is a rather sophisticated tool, and you will need the help of a good investment advisor. That brings us to the next consideration.

Do I Need an Advisor?

The Internet has opened up the investing world to everyone. Anyone can go online and open a trading account and buy and sell stocks, bonds, mutual funds, index funds, or REITS. Why would anyone still pay an advisor 1 percent of their investments per year to manage it when they can do it themselves? It is a valid argument. After all, you could automatically have 15 percent of your income go into a 401(k) account invested in and S&P index fund, and never underperform the market, right?

The answer really comes down to

- **How educated are you?**
- **How emotional are you?**
- **How disciplined are you?**

Do you need help to determine your investment strategy, or are you educated enough to do it yourself? Are you emotional enough to jump out of an investment when it goes south like the S&P did in 2008, or jump into day trading because your friend hit it big on a one-day trade, earning more than your 401(k) did all year? Or are you disciplined enough to stick to your strategy, recognizing that the tortoise will always beat the hare in the long run, and that the only person who gets hurt is the one who jumps off of the roller coaster, not the ones who rides it until the end!

Bottom line is that I have found very few people who are where they need to be in all three of these areas, and therefore, good advisors will usually more than payoff in the long run.

How Do I Find a "Good" Advisor?

The easiest answer is to start with the list of things you *don't* want in an advisor.

1. If he or she tries to get you to invest inside an insurance product: There is nothing good about investing within an insurance product unless you are the insurance salesman receiving the commissions from these lousy investment vehicles. The only exception might be variable annuities that allow for good investment returns but put a floor on losses for certain investors who need that protection.

2. If he or she acts as though he or she has an inside track on a surefire moneymaking scheme: *run!* There is nothing new under the sun. If an investment does not have a long track record, it is likely very high risk. Anyone who wants you to take that kind of risk with anything but a very small percentage (less than 10 percent) of your investment is likely not trustworthy.
3. If he or she advises you to invest anything more than 10 percent of your nest egg in individual stocks.
4. If you leave a meeting feeling like you were being "sold to."

The last part of the answer is to make sure your advisor is knowledgeable and has the heart of a teacher. You should never invest in anything you do not understand, and the advisor's only job is to teach you about your options so that you can choose your investments with confidence that they are right for you, your situation, and your goals.

Investment Recommendations

I will tell you that I personally have had a financial advisor for the last fifteen years, and I strongly believe that he has been extremely effective in helping me to learn and especially to take a reasoned, disciplined approach to investing rather than emotionally jumping in and out of the market, or to jump into individual stocks, or even get involved in day trading. Many of these options have been chased by my peers, and I am not aware of any that are in a position of financial freedom before the age of fifty-five except me, despite the fact that my average salary for my thirty-five-year career is only about $75,000. Many of my peers have done much better on the income side of the equation. Further, I did not start investing until almost a decade into my career, and then only started with 4 percent of my income, and increased at 1 percent per year out of my raises from there until I reached 15 percent of my income.

Up until this year, my investments consisted of a fully paid-off primary residence and stock mutual funds. My mutual funds were spread across four types: growth, growth-and-income, aggressive growth, and international. Recently, I converted to a passive investing strategy using ETFs that are designed to match the market performance. We will discuss active versus passive investing shortly. Most of my existing investments are in tax-favored retirement accounts, with as much as possible being in Roth accounts that will grow tax-free.

This strategy has worked very well for me, and my financial advisor has worked with me as life has progressed to put this plan into motion and keep it on track. Through adjusting income, changing life goals, and fluid family situations he has been a voice of wisdom, with the heart of a teacher, in my corner.

Where to Find an Advisor One Can Trust?

If you do not know where you can find an investment advisor like that, I will point you toward two networks of Advisors who have been vetted by people I trust. The first is Dave Ramsey's "SmartVestors" for Investing. You can find them by going to DaveRamsey.com and click on "Dave Recommends" and then "SmartVestor."

Next is a group of Christian professional financial advisors called Certified Kingdom Advisors. This is a network of investment professionals affiliated with trusted author and financial guru, Ron Blue. You can find these professionals at kingdomadvisors.com. I will talk more about Ron Blue and his impact on me and my own journey to Financial Freedom in a later chapter, but I would not hesitate to recommend his network of advisors. I have actually done their core training module and their investing strategies and approaches nicely align with mine.

Both of these resources will link people with a professional who can meet them where they are, see what needs to be done to get them there, and make suggestions based on what will benefit the client, not based on what will benefit the advisor in the form of fees and commissions.

There are two differentiators that might be important when selecting an advisor, even from these trusted sources. One is whether or not their company is an RIA, or registered investment advisor. This designation indicates the company is registered with the Securities and Exchange Commission, or state securities authorities, and have a fundamental obligation (known as *fiduciary duty*) to provide suitable investment advice and always act in their clients' best interests. The same requirement exists for financial advisors who have the certified financial planner (CFP) designation. There were some regulatory moves to make this a requirement of all financial advisors introduced in 2016, but the implementation and enforcement is far from certain as of this writing. Therefore, I would lean toward working with RIAs and or CFPs at this point as they are held to a higher standard.

Active versus Passive Investing Strategy

The simplest definition for this differentiation is whether or not one is trying to "beat the market." There are various levels of risk for people who try to beat the market, starting at the high end with day traders and junk bond investors, down to the low end with people who use stock and bond mutual funds to try to outpace the S&P. After years of besting the market with a diversified mutual fund strategy, my mutual funds started to be outpaced by the S&P the last few years. This caused me to look at my holdings over the last fifteen years and realize that over that period I had actually underperformed the market in total, especially when I took into account that I could reduce my financial advisor fees by more than 1 percent ($10,000/year if you have $1 million invested) if I went to a passive investing strategy. That 1 percent is guaranteed regardless of market performance because whether your investments go up or go down, your broker still gets paid. There is a great *Wall Street Journal* article from April 15, 2017, entitled "Why Passive Investing is Overrunning Active," in Five Charts, that backs up my decision. A very small percentage of mutual funds outperform index funds and the fees for this less-than-market-average advising are a lot higher.

The bottom line is that I believe I have become educated enough and disciplined enough to overcome any emotional challenges with a volatile market. My financial advisor and I agreed it was the right move for me at this stage in my life. It is not for everyone, but I think it is something to move toward over time when one is at the point that her advisor does not have to talk her off the ledge with every market correction, or talk him out of taking 50 percent of his retirement out to invest in his sister's start-up venture.

Baby Step 5

Invest for your children's education, utilizing tax-favored retirement accounts.

Many of the investing lessons from the retirement section will apply to this arena as well. First, there are two tax-favored vehicles available for people who are saving for education. Educational Savings Accounts and 529 Plans. Both are after-tax investing vehicles that then grow tax-free. Both must be used for higher education and have penalty and tax implications if they are taken out for any other purpose, so it is very important to brainwash your kids that they will be going on for higher education. Otherwise you will lose the tax sheltering benefit on the amount saved.

Next, the sooner you start, the more time you will have for compounding interest to work for you. The overall horizon is only eighteen years compared to forty or so for retirement, so your risk tolerance, especially as the children become teenagers, may be quite different than your retirement accounts unless you have other accessible cash flow or investments to help you weather any downturn on the investments.

Finally, be sure to remember all the lessons in the "Picking Your Track" section about college choice. Work with your kids to pick a degree with market relevance and to find a career that ignites one's passion. Without these lessons, all the money invested in this arena could be wasted.

Baby Step 6

Pay off the mortgage on your primary residence.

For most of us, the largest single asset we will own in our lifetime is our house. According to Zillow.com the median home price in the United States at the penning of these words is $184,600. According to CNN, the typical family's average income in the United States was $53,647 in 2015, meaning that the average family would have to invest three years of earnings to own their home outright. This is no easy task. In fact, less than 30 percent of homeowners own their home outright. The rest have mortgages. Is it really realistic to pay off your home? Is it important to even try?

Let me answer the second question first. Yes, it is important to pay off your home. Why? Because after you pay off your mortgage if you come home, take off your shoes and walk through the grass in your backyard, the ground under your feet will feel different because you *own it!* It is *yours.* No one else has a claim to it!

I can testify to this personally. My wife and I paid off our mortgage in 2015. Afterward, we walked out into the backyard with no shoes on. Karen took a picture of our bare feet with her phone and had it printed on a mug and gave it to me for Christmas because it is one of our best memories, evoking one of the best feelings I have ever had in my life. At the time we did this, our net worth was well over $1 million, but I never felt fully free financially while I owed someone hundreds of thousands of dollars on my house. So we made the decision to sell a rental house we owned outright and use the proceeds to pay off our primary residence.

Many financial advisors would have thought this to be foolish. They would have pointed out that I could take the $225,000 from the sale of the rental and invest it in mutual funds with an expected return of 10 percent versus the 3.75 percent interest savings that I was sure to get by paying off the mortgage. That is like walking away from $14,000 per year earnings. The math nerd in me knows they are correct, but I know I made the right decision in spite of the math.

First, the calculation above does not factor in risk. What if the stock market plummets and my $220,000 turns into $110,000? What if the housing market tanks again, right when I have a job loss and I am upside down on my mortgage? What if both of those happen at the same time? (Think 2008–2009!) If I take these advisors advice I could be a victim of a double hit. Since I have no mortgage, I made 3.75 percent on my money, and I can ride out *any* job loss or economic downturn! I will trade $14,000 per year for that peace any day of the week.

Second, this level of freedom opens the world up to me. I can choose to leave my job and work from home, starting my own business. I can take a commission only job with a consulting firm and travel the world with my wife. I can move to Hilton Head (my favorite place on the planet!) and retire. I can do whatever I want because I owe *no one* anything! This freedom almost always leads to better choices with greater financial returns than ones where one has to figure out how to pay on debts in the midst of these opportunities.

I may not be able to throw it on a spreadsheet today and prove that paying off my house was the best financial move, but I have no doubt that one day in the future I will be able to do so. Try it, and you will experience the same security and freedom as I have. If you do not agree that it is the best choice, you can always go get another mortgage!

CHAPTER 7

Keeping on Track (By Always Having an Income)

As we pointed out in the last chapter, it is a long journey from Normal to Millionaire Mountain, and you have to keep fueling the engine by investing 15 percent of your income into retirement accounts until you max out what is allowed in those types of investment vehicles, and then into nonsheltered vehicles, such as real estate or mutual funds. It is important to note that 15 percent of nothing is still nothing, so protecting your income stream will be essential to keeping your train's engine fueled for the long haul.

Things have changed immensely in the baby boom generation when it comes to career. I was born in 1962, and I saw my mom and stepfather work for decades at the same employer and retire with a comfortable middle-class pension. (My father, on the other hand, died destitute at fifty-nine as I stated previously). I headed off to college in the fall of 1980, and before I was well established in my career, that whole model was made irrelevant. Mergers and acquisitions were happening left and right in the eighties and large cash-heavy pension funds became chips traded from workers to shareholders in the form of investable liquid assets. A study by the Employee Benefit Research Institute showed that in 1979 62 percent of companies offered only pension plans, and only 16 percent offered

401(k)-type plans alone. In 2011, that has totally been reversed, with 69 percent offering only 401(k)-type plans and only 7 percent offering pension plans alone.

In the 1990s the emergence of the Internet forever changed the competitive landscape of business, opening up the world for new online marketing, and accessing labor from third world countries for pennies on the dollar versus labor costs in the United States. Companies have continued to reduce fixed labor in favor of outsourced-as-needed labor, and major portions of the workforce seldom if ever come to a brick-and-mortar location to do their jobs. Gallup reported in 2015 that 37 percent of the US workforce said they did some telecommuting, up from 30 percent in 2005 and 9 percent in 1995. The net effect of this portability of labor has been a downward pressure on wages in the United States and much less stability for people in their careers. According to *Forbes* magazine in an article published in 2012, the average person now changes jobs every 4.4 years, but the tenure of millennials is expected to be about half of that, resulting in a reality where workers will have fifteen to twenty jobs over the course of their careers.

That amount of change brings huge risk that there will be gaps in your employment. Those gaps will not only result in lack of fuel for your train to continue toward Financial Freedom but may also cause you to have to utilize your savings to live on, which will result in you having to move backward on your track. Further, if you fall in the trap of utilizing debt in those situations, it may well send you on a one-way express ride back to Normal, where you will have to start the journey all over again!

Keeping an emergency fund in place will give you a cushion, but it may not, in itself, prevent you from being derailed. I have found the following six strategies to be indispensable for never having a break in income. That is not to say I have no risk. Only that, so far, I have successfully mitigated my risk and been able to stay gainfully employed ever since I was fifteen years old.

Six Strategies to Stay Gainfully Employed

1. **Be a Linchpin:** Seth Godin, in his book *Linchpin*, summed up what you have to do in this new age to achieve the American dream this way: "Do you remember the old American dream? It struck a chord with millions of people (in the United States and in the rest of the world, too). Here's how it goes: Keep your head down, follow instructions, show up on time, work hard, and suck it up ... you will be rewarded. As we've seen, that dream is over. The new American dream, though, the one that markets around the world are embracing as fast as they can, is this: Be remarkable, be generous, create art, make judgment calls, and connect people and ideas."

   In short, you have to be creative, brilliant, serve, and succeed. Oh, and by the way, it does not matter what you did last year, or this morning for that matter. What you can do tomorrow and next year is the only thing that makes you indispensable! There is no resting on past achievements in this new model. You have to bring it, day in and day out; never tiring and never falling short.

   This is why it so important to pick the right track, and the right type of train. If you are not passionate and committed, you will never be a linchpin, and that will place you always at risk. If you are always at risk, you will be stressed out and miserable, which will cause you to be more ineffective and more vulnerable. The downward spiraling effect conjures images that will flush your career and, with it, your progress on the journey from Normal to Millionaire Mountain.

2. **Build or Rehab Your Brand:** I learned this lesson a few years ago. Everyone should have a personal mission statement. Most people who do not make good decisions with their lives and their careers mess up because they do not really understand who it is they are and what it is they want to

accomplish with their lives. A personal mission statement is a synthesis of all those things and thereby can be used like a compass when you come to a fork in the tracks and you need to decide which one you should take.

This mission statement should also be used to assess whether others' perceptions of you line up with what you mean to project. If so, *fantastic!* If not, well you have some work to do. I found myself in this position a few years ago. I clarified my personal mission statement thus: "I am a servant leader helping us implement common sense principles for lasting impact." The issue was many people did not see the "servant" in my leadership style nearly as much as I wished they did. Further, many of them also did not necessarily believe that some of the ideas I promoted were necessarily "common sense." When people do not recognize your mission statement in what they see, it is time to be about the business of making it obvious.

There are many ways to build or rehab your personal brand, but it really is about putting your priorities in place when it comes to your time, energy, and checking account. You can say whatever you want about yourself, but others will recognize you by your calendar, your check register, and the relationships you have in your life. If those things do not create an image in line with your personal mission, then reprioritize so the reflection you see in the eyes of others will be what you intended.

In my situation I looked for more opportunities to serve. I led small groups at my church, volunteered for a nonprofit board, took on committee roles at work, and poured into the people who worked under my oversight so they could grow and advance. I also looked for opportunities to teach about what I believe are common sense strategies for success that have become less common in our society, which caused me to start writing books and blogs to share the wisdom I have garnered from others and benefited from in my life's journey.

The result is that I believe that others see my life in my personal mission statement and my personal mission statement in my life. I do not walk it out perfectly, but I believe there is a recognizable continuity of which I am now proud to live out. This is important to maintaining gainful employment. Duplicity breeds distrust, and distrust leads to displacement. Engender trust and you are much more likely to survive the downsizings that are largely inevitable in the shifting markets of today's global economy.

3. **Be A Servant:** This may be the most important strategy of all for staying gainfully employed. First, if you serve others well people will want to keep you around out of their own self-interest. If I have two employees in a similar job function, and one does great work and brings more value to the company than they take, while a second one does the same but also offers to assist me when I have a special project, which one will I keep when the downturn comes and I have no option but to let someone go, it's a no-brainer. I take the one who goes the extra mile to help me!

Secondly, servants are just more likable. People want them around because they make everyone's life easier. For those of you who watch *Survivor* on CBS, you see this all the time. For those not familiar with the show, every week someone gets voted off whatever island the show resides on this season until there are three left. Then the jury votes for one of the three to be the sole survivor who wins $1 million. The first people who get voted off the show are the lazy people who just hang around and eat the tribe's food while others build the shelter, catch the food, fetch water, fetch wood, and build the fire to boil the water and cook the food. The servants who provide for the tribe are kept around a lot longer, until the end of the game when people realize that those servants are so well liked that they will win the million, then they try to vote them off, but often it is too late. By then they have forged alliances with people because people like them and like to be around them. Occasionally, a snake will win *Survivor*, but more often than not, it as a servant who wins the game.

The game of life is usually the same. Takers may win for a while, but in the long run the givers win. Serving well has served me well in life.

4. **Be a Networker:** There are people who are much better than I am at this skill, but I work at it, and I am continuing to become better at it. A networker is a person who connects people to:
   - other people;
   - resources they may need;
   - opportunities they would like; and
   - wisdom that will help them achieve their wildest dreams!

The best example of this is a friend of mine named Steve. Steve is one of those guys who knows everyone, and everyone knows Steve. He was a chiropractor for thirty years and hugely successful, but in his fifties he experienced an injury that would not allow him to continue to perform the strenuous duties of practicing chiropractic medicine. He was the perfect candidate to experience the huge gap in income that would cause a return trip to Normal, erode retirement savings and take on debt until he could retrain and start generating income from a new skill set. Instead he looked at what he had created in his career and recognized the value he had brought to his patients and also the value that he had brought to many medical professionals.

He realized that he had a tremendous opportunity to organize other chiropractors into a network that would bring enormous numbers of referrals to hospitals and other medical specialists, such as spine surgeons, pain clinics, imaging centers, and orthopedic surgeons. He knew that chiropractors were undervalued and even maligned by the medical community that benefited from their referrals. He had often struggled to get his patients seen by medical specialists, particularly if they were injured in an accident that was covered by liability insurance instead of traditional medical insurance, even though the reimbursement per case was often better than that from a managed care insurer.

His results have been remarkable! He has established several networks in Atlanta, New York, Savannah, and Baton Rouge, totaling over five thousand chiropractors working with dozens of hospitals, imaging centers, surgery centers, and medical surgical subspecialty physician groups to offer integrated care to these previously underserved patients.

What is the cost to be a member of this network? Nothing. Not a dollar. The value is in the relationships he has created by connecting these disparate groups and the referrals that come out of mutual respect for each other's roles and skill sets. He has come out fine in the equation as the consultant hired to create these collaborative networks.

5. **Build a Side Income:** As you gain experience, leverage it in the market by creating income from consulting, writing, teaching, or something else. This helps you assure you will always have a parachute on if you are pushed out of the plane by an employer. The landing is always less painful and less damaging if you have a parachute. This is not as necessary if you picked the entrepreneurial express train, or switched to one of those along the journey. With that vehicle you typically already have multiple income streams as you usually have multiple clients.

With a traditional job, you essentially have one client. That client has way too much power if you do not create another stream of income they do not control. Eventually your investment nest egg will give you that, but not for a decade or two will it likely be material. In the meantime, look for opportunities to create side income. If you are prohibited from doing it in the field you work in, look into starting an eBay or Craigslist business, or turn a hobby you love into a side job. Or maybe you could be an online professor teaching Millennials how to come replace you in your day job when your side job overtakes the income your day job!

6. **Plan for Transitions:** Be aware of your workplace culture and environment. The landscape of your journey can shift dramatically in no time with a change in management team, a merger or acquisition, a poor financial outlook resulting in reductions in force. Sometimes you can do everything you can to be a linchpin but still be left out in the cold by an employer at the end of the day. Other times you may see them coming. In one instance, you may receive a severance package; in the next you may be handed a pink slip out of the blue one Friday afternoon or even arrive to a padlocked office door one morning because the company has closed and filed for bankruptcy. The moral of the story is that you should always plan on the next transition. Here are some tips to be prepared:

- Keep your resume fresh and up to date. Did you lead a project at your current employer, hit a major goal, or win an award for leadership? Update your resume and LinkedIn profiles with that information so people who need good people see what you have been up to in your current role.
- Keep a current list of favorable references and keep in contact with them. You never know when a recruiter may call you with an offer that is too good to ignore, even if you are happy as a clam at your current gig. Do not get caught having to scramble for current contact info from your old bosses. Keep up with them and

keep their contact information at hand. Further, always contact them when you list them as a reference so they will not be caught off guard when someone calls them.
- Make an effort to help recruiters. Recruiters are great people. They help people reach their goals and achieve their dreams. If one reaches out to you and it is a position you are not interested in, make sure you offer to send it on to other members of your network who might be! Be a networker. Also tell them what you might be interested in if they come across it.
- Look for opportunities to take on more and save your company more. I have been very successful finding opportunities to get promotions or upgrade hiring managers offers through taking on more responsibility and eliminating a salaried position in the process. Look for those opportunities when teammates leave or new product/service lines are being added. It serves two purposes for you. It brings more income in the short run and makes you more indispensable in the long run.
- Make sure you raise up leaders who can take your place when you move on. This may seem counterintuitive to maintaining job security, but I am convinced that it has benefited me in the long run. When you reach out to past employers for references, you will be glad you did this. If you leave the organization in a position to keep moving forward after you are gone, you will avoid being the scapegoat for things that go wrong because things do not go wrong.

CHAPTER 8

Step 6: Look at the Landscape

You make it back to your sleep car after another long day of fueling the engine. You are tired. I mean really tired. "How long have I been at this?" you wonder. It seems like an eternity of days shoveling coal in those dirty overalls. You can tell you are getting closer to Millionaire Mountain because it keeps getting bigger and bigger as you move toward it, but honestly, it seems like it will be many years to get there at this rate, and you start to wonder, "Is it really worth it?"

Just then, the black-clad conductor comes walking down the aisle with his gold pocket watch opened in his hand. "We are making good time, young man!" he says with a smile.

You muster enough energy and civility to smile faintly and respond, "Thanks," but it comes out more like a groan as every muscle in your body feels sore and spent.

"What's this now? Do I sense someone is feeling a little discouraged?" the conductor asks.

"I don't know about this journey," you reply. "It seems like such a long way to go, and I am not sure it is worth it."

"Well, I am not surprised," the conductor states. "All you have done is kept your head down and shoveled coal day in and day out for about as long as I can remember."

"Isn't that what I am supposed to do? You told me that I needed to constantly fuel the engine with coal to get to Millionaire Mountain, and like you said, we are making good progress, right? What is it you want from me!"

"What is it I want from you?" the conductor asks. "I only want to help you make your journey. It is your journey, and only you can make it. I did say you needed to consistently fuel the engine, not constantly. Most people cannot keep up the pace that you have set since you started. It is like trying to sprint your way through a marathon—people are just not built to do that."

"It just seems so futile," you state. "I mean this looks like it is going to take me years! I am beginning to wonder if I was not better off in Normal! At least there I had fun and friends to share my life with."

"Why don't you have fun and friends on this journey with you?" the conductor asks.

"I did not know that was allowed," you answer.

"As I said before, this is your journey and your train. "There is plenty of room for many more passengers. All you have to do is look at the landscape around you on the journey, and you will see sights and meet people who can give you the richest of lives you could imagine! You have just had your head down shoveling coal all the time, which is fine if that is what you want, but if you want to engage with the world around you, take a look outside. I guarantee you never saw things like this in Normal!"

So then you look out the window, and it's as if scales have been lifted from your eyes. Suddenly there is a world filled with vibrant colors, teeming with life all around you. Flocks of birds fill the azure sky. Herds of grazing animals are everywhere, as well as sleek predators lying in wait to hunt them. In the distance, schools of porpoises break the surface of a river that flows into the bluest of oceans, waves crashing against the rocky cliffs, shooting fountains of water through blow holes hundreds of feet into the sky!

"The world is a remarkably abnormal place," the conductor says softly, shaking you back to the reality of the sleep car. "You could press on through, day in and day out, pushing to Millionaire Mountain at breakneck speed, but if you think you should enjoy the journey a little more than you have been, just look out at the landscape. When you see something you want to get closer to, just stop the train, go take a walk and live in the landscape for a while. The journey to Millionaire Mountain is a joy to be lived, not a chore to be dreaded."

You look back out the window, and in the distance you see another train stopped on a parallel track. Next to the train is the most beautiful woman you have ever seen, frantically waving her arms, while jumping up and down.

"Stop the train!" you shout, and instantly your train starts to slow to a stop so that the entrance to the passenger car is directly in front of the beautiful woman. You rush through the sleep car to greet her. You get to the entrance as she steps through, a vision of beauty. You welcome her with a smile and a kind, extended hand of greeting. In that moment you realize your hand, as the rest of you, is covered in grime and soot.

"Welcome to my train," you say sheepishly.

"Thanks so much for stopping!" Her voice was the sweetest sound your ears had ever heard. "Many other trains went right by me as though they did not see me."

"I'm so glad I was looking," you reply.

The conductor appeared just then. "Will you be joining us for a while then, ma'am?"

"Yes, if that is all right? I am afraid my train is beyond repair. I will have to build another one at the next stop" she replied.

"Build another one?" you ask, and only then do you notice that the broken-down train is one of those sleek, bullet-shaped ones like you saw at the train station on Hope Hill back in Normal. "An Entrepreneurial Express," you say almost under your breath, somewhat in awe. "Did you build that in Normal?"

"Yes, a couple of weeks ago, but apparently I did not get it quite right," she responds.

"You got here from Normal in a couple of weeks? I have been traveling for years!"

"Well, right now I am thinking you are the smart one," she muses.

"If it were not for you, I would be stranded in the wilderness. You and your train are in the right place and at the right time for me!"

The conductor then gives you a knowing look and states, "The right place at the right time indeed, without a doubt. The right place and the right time for all involved." He then walks away, and you and the lovely lady sit down and begin to talk and share, and dream. You continue to talk as you head to the engine together, shoveling coal into the engine for hours, and then return to the dining car for dinner, and for hours after the meal, you lose yourself in conversation. By the end of the evening, you are standing together on the back of the caboose, witnessing beautiful shooting stars falling across the plains. Gone are all thoughts about returning to Normal.

Financial freedom is not the total picture of success. It is only one slice.

The best tool I have seen to help make sure my life stays in balance as I pursue my financial goals is Zig Ziglar's "Wheel of Life" from his book *Born to Win*. It is a tool that Zig recommended in goal setting. I see Zig's model as a forerunner to a trend that is in vogue right now; creating a life plan:

As you can see in Zig's model, *financial* is an identified area for goal setting for success, but there are six other areas he taught need to be taken into consideration in order for people to really have "successful" lives. Not having these areas all well rounded will result in a flat-tire effect that will prevent you from getting where you want to go!

As you are well aware by this point, this book addresses the financial section of the wheel in detail. While I am not able to go into that same level of detail for the other important areas of life, I think it is important to address all six of them so that you understand how they relate to successfully traveling from Normal to Millionaire Mountain and the land of Financial Freedom beyond.

Family

Family dynamics will greatly impact one's ability to accumulate wealth. This starts with marriage. Thomas J. Stanley, PhD, in his book *The Millionaire Mind,* said that his research shows a strong correlation with length of marriages and wealth of households. Part of this has to do with the realities of divorce and impact to household wealth. First, it splits assets in half, and then a significant portion also goes to legal fees in addition to that split. Therefore, it is natural that we find more millionaire households with marriage longevity. Stanley says that the correlation does not totally rely upon the math of divorce, however. His research showed that for every 100 millionaires who said that support of a spouse is not an important factor to accumulating wealth, 1,317 said their spouse was an important factor. This came up so frequently in the research that "A Supportive Spouse" came up as one of the five foundation stones of financial success according to Dr. Stanley's research.

My own personal experience puts me in the camp of the 1,317. Though my wife only worked outside the home a few years of our thirty-year marriage, I know we would not be millionaires if it were not for her. She is the one who started us saving for retirement in our twenties, starting at 4 percent and adding 1 percent per year out of raises. She was more debt averse than me and certainly a thriftier shopper than I was. We have worked on a budget together for over twenty years, and because we have used that tool, we have never had a serious disagreement over money. The number-one cause of divorce is money fights and money problems, and we were able to eliminate those by being on the same page about our finances.

Mental (Intellectual)

Dr. Stanley's research about millionaires sheds some interesting light on this subject as well. The average GPA for the millionaires he studied was 2.92 on a four-point scale. The richest of those millionaires were ones who owned their own businesses, and the average GPA of that group was only 2.76. That is a C to C-plus, in case you did not know. The point is that one can achieve wealth with average intelligence.

Zig Ziglar was a huge proponent of ongoing learning, and he encouraged people to set intellectual goals, such as reading books, attending seminars, and other educational opportunities, and multitasking by turning your car into "Automobile University." In his day that was through cassette tapes, but with today's technology podcasts, TED Talks, online audiobooks, and even online videos on smartphones can turn planes, trains, and automobiles into enough higher education to take you to any intellectual height you want to attain at very little or even no cost

Another trait identified by Dr. Stanley as a foundation stone is *discipline*. Though his research did not show a need for high GPA, it did show a need to be disciplined which when applied to this area will propel people to further success.

Work

We covered quite a bit on how to succeed at work in an earlier chapter, but I wanted to once again talk about Dr. Stanley's research to dispel some myths about what a millionaire does for a living. Only 9 percent of millionaires were doctors, and 10 percent were lawyers. Only 16 percent were senior corporate executives. The largest group of millionaires was business owners/entrepreneurs at 32 percent. That leaves 33 percent that were "other." Other professionals, other laborers, other clerks, and other call center operators. They are just average Joes and Janes who worked hard and invested in 401(k)s, IRAs, and their homes to become millionaires. The bottom line is that one can do almost any kind of work and become a millionaire if she is intentional. This is why Dr. Stanley identified *hard work* as another of his foundation stones.

Social

The last two of Dr. Stanley's five foundation stones relate to this area. They are

- **Integrity**—being honest with all people; and
- **Social Skills**—getting along with people.

A growing body of research is emerging that demonstrates this is quite probably the most important area to achieving success in business and, therefore, being able to consistently fund your investments by maintaining an income. Corporations are investing millions in various survey tools that help determine if candidates are good personality- and communication-style fits with a given organizational culture or even for specific roles in an organization. They are employing the tools in the screening process so that even if your resume looks like a perfect fit, you may never get an interview if you do not meet the personality guidelines for which they are looking.

Invest time in learning how to relate to bosses, coworkers, and subordinates. Invest time and energy in those relationships. Finally, remember the ultimate guidance for winning in relationships. It works almost every time. You heard it in kindergarten and or Sunday school. Let's all say it together: "Treat others like you would want to be treated." The Golden Rule is still the gold standard for great relationships.

Physical

The vast majority of millionaires are made over decades through hard work and savings. Maintaining health is necessary for that long haul. Then, if they are to enjoy the fruits of their labor in retirement or in a second-act career, health will be of utmost importance.

Our society worships at the altar of fitness and health, but like people who are in church on Sundays with hangovers from bar hopping on Saturday night, we pay homage to health and fitness by hanging our clothes on our StairMasters, eat what we shouldn't, and exercise very little. The result is that we are the unhealthiest generation in history. Couple that with the fact that medical advances have us living longer than ever, and the result could mean that the only people who benefit from our journey to Millionaire Mountain are assisted-living facilities, nursing homes, and our heirs!

It does not have to be that way. Small steps done daily can enable any of us to move into fitness so we can enjoy our hard-earned golden years.

Spiritual

I am a Christian, and everything that is important in my life is tied to my connection with my Creator and a desire to bring honor and glory to Him. No matter what your personal belief system is, I am convinced that personal success can only take you so far. Unless you connect to a greater purpose than making yourself happy, the depth of your success will leave you wanting. Without the acknowledgement of a higher power, we have no way to orient our lives other than what makes us happy today. We humans are fickle. What we enjoy today may bore us tomorrow. That applies to hobbies, desserts, and spouses. Living for what pleases us today will leave a wake of destruction in our lives and ultimately result in an unfulfilling life filled only with regret.

If, however, you believe in an all-knowing, all-powerful, loving God who has a plan for your life to bless you and make you a blessing to the world around you, it will simultaneously rein you in and set you free. In my world view, spirituality is not about ritual; it is about a relationship with the Creator. Like all relationships, you have to invest time and energy and make sure you keep the lines of communication open. For me that means time for prayer and scripture reading has to be a priority. When I make it so, I stay connected. When I do not, I know that I still have a relationship, but it is not all it can be. Having goals in this arena, and hitting them seems to have a positive impact in all the other areas. It is an exponential effect.

Balance Is the Key

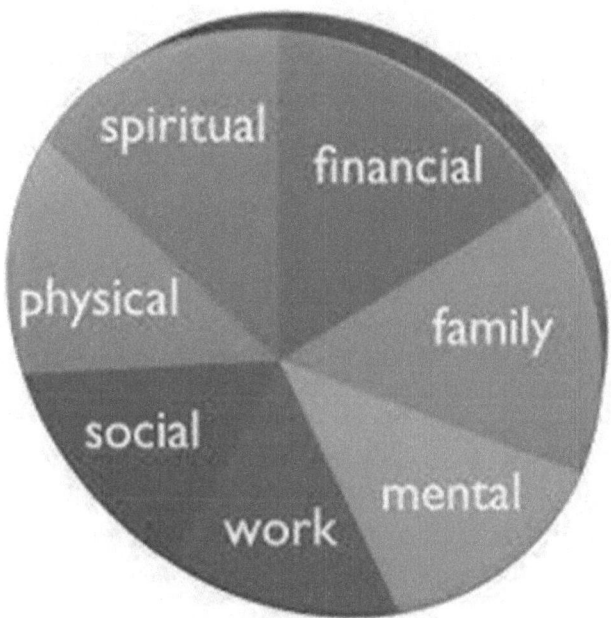

Everyone's life is composed of these elements, whether we choose to acknowledge them or not. It is very easy to identify people who completely ignore certain aspects of their lives, whether it is financial recklessness, workaholics ignoring family responsibilities, or people who ignore their health and poison their bodies with junk food, alcohol, and cigarettes. The reality is that most people try to have a good life and expend some effort in all of these areas. What separates those who have joy, peace, and happiness from those who do not?

At the risk of alienating some people with different spiritual paradigms, I am going to answer with some wisdom I have gleaned from the New Testament of the Bible. In fact, I will use a story recounted about a conversation that Jesus himself had with a young man who seemed to have the world by the tail. Yet this young man came to Jesus seeking more. You can read the story for yourself in chapter 19 of the book of Matthew. The young man asked Jesus what he must do to have eternal life. Jesus recited a list of commands from the Ten Commandments that had to do with how we should treat other people. The young man responded that he had observed all of these since he was a boy. Then Jesus agreed, saying that he had indeed done so, but told him there was one more thing he must do to be perfect: sell all he had and give it to the poor, and come follow Jesus. When the young man heard Jesus's commands, the Scripture tells us, "He went away sorrowful, for he had great possessions."

There are two important lessons from this story. The first one is a theological lesson. If you look at the remainder of the Ten Commandments, they have to do with how one should relate with God. The young man had kept all the commandments about how he should relate to other people, but his possessions had become his idols, in direct violation of the commandment, "Thou shalt have no other gods before me." His unwillingness to let go of his possessions and follow this man he clearly believed to be a great prophet and teacher exposed that fact. Later in this same New Testament book of Matthew, Jesus summed up all of the Law and the writings of the Old Testament prophets into only two commandments: the greatest—love the Lord your God with all your heart, with all your soul, and all your mind, and the second—love your neighbor as yourself.

The rich, young man had done the latter, but he had forsaken the former. He no longer owned his possessions; the possessions owned him, keeping him from the very thing he had sought his entire life—eternal life with the God of his forefathers. Earlier in the same book of Matthew, Jesus had taught his followers to "seek first the Kingdom of God, and His righteousness, and all the other things (food, clothing … stuff) will be added unto you" (Matthew 6:33). The rich, young man had gained the lesser, but lost the greater.

Choose the Experience, Not the Stuff

The second lesson is a practical lesson regardless of your belief system. The rich, young ruler had a practical decision in front of him. Should he keep his stuff, or should he forgo it in favor of the experience of a lifetime? It is a practical lesson regarding a decision we face every day in this consumer-driven, marketing-inundated society. We are sold that stuff will make us happy. We rent too nice an apartment or buy too much house on debt. We buy cars, boats, campers, and Jet Skis that all go down in value, usually on debt, with the only decision factor being that we can make the monthly payments. Even school loans factor in, because we are sold that regardless of what it costs, this is the only path to get the job with the big salary so we can buy all the stuff we *need* to make us happy. My personal experience in fifty-four years of life, and an abundant amount of psychological research over the last decade, have supported the reality that money is better spent on experiences than stuff, if you want to be happy.

I believe there are some very commonsense reasons for this. First is the anticipation factor. When planning an experience, there is almost always an element of time involved that forces us to wait and anticipate. The anticipation builds the excitement over a longer period of time so that it extends the happiness or excitement felt over a longer period than ordering something on Amazon for next-day shipping or going to a store and buying something. Why is Christmas most people's favorite holiday? It is the whole season of preparation and shopping, wrapping and shaking the gifts under the tree. It is the buildup, or crescendo, that ends on Christmas morning. Once we have the stuff it is actually a bit of a letdown. How many of you have noticed that the toys you buy your kids on Christmas are largely unused after January?

Another reason is that most experiences we purchase involve other people and therefore affect many areas on our wheel of life. Family and friends are often included, touching on the family and social component. We are often doing physical things together, which touches another component. It might even be a service project done with a small group of friends or family that involves using our work skill sets for the betterment of others, bringing in the spiritual aspect through serving. The more areas of the wheel of life we impact, the more meaningful and impactful the experience is to our overall success in achieving life balance.

Practical Tips Regarding Buying Stuff (To Leave More Money for Buying Experiences)

Housing: Whether you are buying or renting limit your payment to 25 percent of your take-home pay, and if you are buying using a mortgage, do so using a fixed-rate mortgage for no longer than fifteen years. With rent, limiting the amount you spend is obvious. Rent builds no equity, so it is logical to limit it. And do not justify doubling the rent for the neighborhood swim, tennis, and fitness center!

It is not as obvious to people when discussing home purchase, where conventional wisdom is to buy as much house as you "can afford" because it is an appreciating asset, and you are gaining some equity with every payment. The banks, which only make money on interest you pay, will encourage you to take out a thirty-year mortgage so you can buy "more house" and will finance you up to 50 percent of your take-home pay. If you follow the banks advice, you will be "house poor," with little room in your budget for experiences in the short run, and over the life of a mortgage on an average home in the United States, you will have spent over $100,000 more in interest than my suggested strategy. A hundred grand could buy a lot of experiences!

Cars, Boats, RVs, and Others

Buy Used. According to Carfax.com cars lose an average of 60 percent of their value in the first five years, the first two years of which are at 15-25 percent per year! This means if you buy a $20,000 new car you are going to pay up to $10,000 for the privilege of owning that car for the first two years. Since the average expected life of a car is currently 8 years per Consumer Reports, you could have bought the same car 2 years later and paid $10,000 for the right to drive it the next 6 years, cutting the amount spent per year of use in one-third.

Buy with Cash. Car loans and leases are extremely profitable for the car dealers. The interest rates are high and there are rich in fees and other "gotchas." Buying with cash will eliminate all those costs, but will also cause you to think about the total cost of ownership instead of "how much down, and how much per month" mentality. That mentality has done more to take away hope in the American dream than any foreign terrorist or corrupt politician. Buy with cash and take back control of your finances and your future.

- **Keep Total Value of Things with Engines at Less than 50 percent of Your Annual Take-Home Pay.** Everything with an engine is a depreciating asset. Every dollar spent on a depreciating asset takes your financial future the opposite direction from what you want. This rule of thumb allows you plenty of room to address your transportation needs and, as you grow your wealth and income, even allows you to get some toys with motors as well.
- **Don't Justify Additional Spending in this Category.** Boats, RVs, Jet Skis, snowmobiles, four-wheelers, and other toys are fun! Surely we can spend more on these, because we can use them to have "experiences," right? If you can

afford them with the guidelines above, I say go for it! If, however, you cannot, then get the experience without the depreciation. There are places that will rent these toys to you and your friends and family to have the "experiences." They will throw in their expertise, maintenance of the vehicles, and the depreciation of them into one daily or weekly price. Until you can truly afford these toys, rent the experience, grow your wealth, and later be free to buy whatever you want!

Furnishings, Jewelry, Collectibles, and Such

These items are expenses. They have almost no chance of appreciating in your lifetime. Some jewelry and antiques may hold their value over time, but it is a crapshoot as to what will and what will not, so never justify buying these items as an investment. The only exception I have seen to this is people who buy these items at estate sales, yard sales, and so on, with the intention of immediately resell for a profit for what they know will sell today. Unless this is a passion and you have researched the market extensively, do not think of these things as anything but an expense line on your budget.

Limits Now, Mean Freedom; Now and Later

If you follow these guidelines regarding buying stuff, you will have room in your budget to buy appropriate experiences. Vacations, cruises, sporting events, mission trips, hobbies, and side businesses will be items you add to your monthly budget planning to afford you the experiences that will make your life rich and meaningful. It will also allow you to pay off your house early, save for your kids' college, and maybe even retire early by becoming a millionaire by fifty-five! As Dave Ramsey puts it, "If you live like no one else, later you can live and give like no one else!"

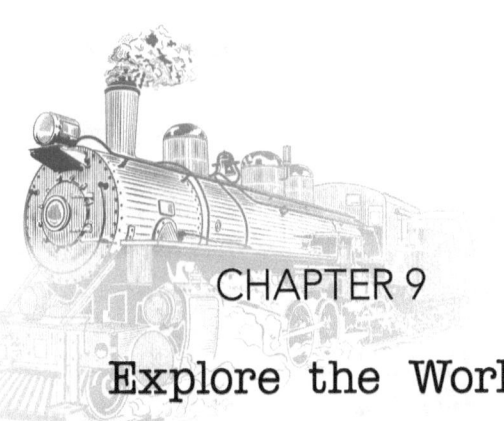

CHAPTER 9

Explore the World

*T*he next years, you explored the world together with the love of your life, raising children, building, driving, and selling a few Entrepreneurial Express trains along the way, quickly replacing them with new ones that ran faster and further. In fact, many others who were journeying to Millionaire Mountain connected their career trains and job trains to your trains, and many later built their own Entrepreneurial Expresses to speed their journeys. You would have probably kept your head down and arrived at Millionaire Mountain a few years earlier, but your love convinced you to take advantage of your faster train to explore more of the world around you. You and your family walked on a thousand beaches, rode zip lines through forests and jungles, hiked through grand canyons, sailed across seven seas. Along the way you met person after person who impacted your lives, some bringing wisdom, kindness, and love, while others caused suffering or suffered themselves due to unspeakable traumas.

You experienced other cultures, some as old as time itself. You saw works of art by the masters from centuries ago, and others on a commercialized fishing pier with thousands of passers-by, seeing them do their work. You played sports with friends, coached sports for your kids, and watched sports in arenas with tens of thousands of other fans, rabid in support of their teams. You enjoyed your life, realizing that the *journey is what is most important, not the goal. You are thankful for the love of your life teaching you that lesson early on.*

Through it all, you grew and so did your family until before you could blink, your children were starting out on their own journeys into the world. You encouraged them and taught them about the things that would benefit them and keep them from returning to Normal. Would they heed your advice? Only time would tell. They had their own journeys to make, determined by their own choices.

Now it is almost that time. You sit by the window holding your true love's hand with the mountain towering before you. In another day, you will have arrived. You will have reached that pinnacle you have been chasing since you decided to leave Normal. You will reach Millionaire Mountain. You are still a young man, or like to think of yourself that way in your early fifties. What will tomorrow hold? What will the land of Financial Freedom on the other side of this peak hold for you?

At that moment, the conductor approaches. "You two should get some rest; you have a big day tomorrow!" So you agree and retire to the sleep car, wondering how anything beyond that mountain could exceed the blessings you have been given in your life thus far.

Going Beyond the Red White and Blue

I love the United States of America. I am true-blue red, white, and blue. I am convinced that this is the greatest country on earth, with freedoms and opportunities that other countries only dream about having. I have experienced different sides of this country from an economic viewpoint. In my childhood I lived in a great starter home in a great up-and-coming area, until my parents divorced and my dad filed bankruptcy and lost it. We then lived in lower-middle-class apartments, and I was bussed into the District of Columbia in the mid-1970s as part of desegregation. A few years later, I moved to my mom's in the foothills of Appalachia, where we still did laundry with a ringer washer and hung the clothes on clotheslines to dry. Now, I am a millionaire! Only in America can this be an everyday occurrence.

Having said that, we in this country can tend to be myopic. Each of us believes that our way is the only right way, and we are dismissive of other cultures and ideas. We have seen that produce strong divides within our own borders and limit our effectiveness beyond them.

It is so easy to travel within the United States, and there is so much beauty and splendor to behold. We have everything from deserts to rainforests, ice-covered tundra to tropical beaches. Our rule of law is consistent, and we pass from state to state without border crossings to slow down our commerce and travel. I hope to be able to see much more of this country before I die, but I also believe, as a people, we need explore the world more.

One of the most meaningful trips of my life was when my boys were thirteen and sixteen, and we went to the Dominican Republic on a mission trip. I had done a similar trip with my wife to the mountains of Mexico when we were first married. On both trips, what struck me was how happy many of the people were despite the fact that they had so few material possessions. We in the United States spend so much time and energy working to pay for all of our stuff. We look at these cultures and see them as unproductive. The communities are filled with gathering places where people meet and talk in the middle of the day. Can you imagine? Why aren't they at work?

In reality they do not have to be at work and earn as much because they are not in debt to their eyeballs. Instead they have time to visit in the heat of the day and work in the mornings and evenings. The people of these communities know each other and care for each other. Their lives are really about relationships instead of obtaining stuff. Are we really so arrogant as to believe our way is better than theirs?

I think everyone in the United States should get outside the United States and experience other cultures. It helped me appreciate the affluence, conveniences, upward mobility, and freedoms of my country. I realized how much we have compared to people in

Jamaica, Haiti, the Dominican Republic, St. Martin, and Mexico, to name a few. But it also caused me to appreciate the attributes of other cultures as well and realize that we need to learn a few things from them.

If you cannot get to these places in person, then get there via the Internet. Raise your international awareness to understand the paradigms of other people around the world, some of which hate America. If we are going to change that mindset, it will not be by guns and bombs and walls. It will be by reaching a hand to them in their times of need with the things they need. We can only do that if we know them. I am not saying there is not a time for war and violence, but I am saying it should be our very last resort. Political partisanship aside, we will only win this war against terror by overcoming evil with good. Our government cannot do it, but we can. Person by person, we can choose to love someone beyond our borders, if we will just lift our eyes beyond our own horizons.

CHAPTER 10

Step 7: Leave a Legacy

*T*he day has finally arrived. You are all packed up and you and your love are atop Millionaire Mountain and disembarking your train for the platform. This platform is like no other you have seen on your travels, however. First, it is a lot less crowded! Your train is alone on a single track with a single departure point. As you step off and look behind you, you can see back down the track you were on, and it is so crystal clear you could almost swear you see Normal. You turn the other way, past the train's locomotive, and you are mesmerized by the most magnificent mountain range that you could ever fathom. The mountains seemed as numerous as the stars, stretching as far as the eye can see to both the left and right in a V shape with this spot being at the point, like the tip of an arrow. Between the mountain ranges lies a beautiful, lush, green valley with rolling hills, crops, orchards, and vineyards. Wild, carnivorous animals nap between herds of herbivores as though death did not have a place in this land.

Your wife lets out an audible sigh at the sight, and you break out of your own trance. The conductor steps up beside you and says, "The land of Financial Freedom." He offers no other comment.

After another minute, you turn to him and ask, "Where do we go from here?"

He replies, "Why anywhere you want of course?"

You chuckle at the response and say, "I know. I know it is our journey, after all!"

"Why exactly correct, sir!" the old conductor replies as though you finally got the punchline to a twenty-five-year-long joke.

You turn to the love of your life and ask, "Well, do you want to go to the left, the right, or straight into the valley?"

"Let's visit the valley first," comes the reply. You both turn and enter the train, but you notice the conductor is staying behind. "Aren't you coming with us?" you ask.

"No, I have been here before, and Lord willing, I will be here again. Many years ago after I lost my one true love, peacefully in that valley, I made the decision to help as many people as I could get out of Normal and make the journey you just made. You were number nine, but I think I have one more in me. Maybe I will see you when I return again."

Just then a train appears on the track ahead, and another platform appears as the train switches from your track to one that materialized out of thin air. "There is my train back to Normal now," says the kind, older man.

Before you can even say goodbye or thank you, the old man dashes to the other train and leaps on as it begins to move. In a blink it disappears, headed back the way you had come.

"I am going to miss him," you say to no one in particular.

There Are Five, and Only Five, Uses of Money

Money is a tool. It is a tool that will be used to **give**, **live**, **guard**, **owe**, and **grow.** Anything you can think of to do with money will fall into one of these categories as we detail below.

Give

To whom much is given, much will be required.

Regardless of religious beliefs, we are all a part of the human race and therefore have a responsibility to each other, if for no other reason than we are the same species! As I pointed out in an earlier chapter, if you make an average salary in the United States, you are in the top 1 percent of income earners in the world. While I do not advocate for wealth redistribution, I do believe in personal responsibility, and we in this society need to look beyond ourselves and care for our fellow humans.

I believe that if we want to have great lives, we have to concentrate outward. If all we do is heap up treasure and experiences for our families and ourselves, then we are missing the things that bring the most joy in life. We have to look for opportunities to contribute, starting where we are and moving out from there. Look for ways you can help those around you, and it does not always take money to do this. For example:

- Do you know a young couple struggling as new parents? Offer to watch the baby so they can have a date night.
- One of your coworkers went out for gall bladder surgery. Organize some friends to bring the family a good meal.
- Be generous to servers at restaurants. They work hard and can only care for their families well when the people they serve treat them with respect by rewarding their hard work with a proper tip.

The world is full of need. It is all around us, and we can meet many of those needs if we will take our eyes off our own selves long enough to see the needs of others. Make this a part of your family's ingrained habits.

Get your teenagers to mow the elderly couple's lawn once every couple of weeks for free. Offer to pick up their groceries when you get yours.

Help out the single mom with a special-needs child by watching the child while she grocery shops.

These are examples of things you can do without lifting your eyes beyond your workplace or your neighborhood. You may not think this effort has that much effect, but imagine our communities if everyone would look for those opportunities and act!

Here are some other ways to impact the world around us after we get our financial houses in order and have excess resources available

Child Sponsorship

One of the most common ways that we can impact people in other countries from the comfort of our homes is to sponsor a child. The sponsorship is usually around $1 a day and provides food, some basic clothing, and education for that child. Over the years, my family has sponsored several children through three different organizations—Compassion International, World Vision, and Holt International. There are many other faith-based and non-faith-based organizations that do tremendous works in this arena.

Funding Missionaries or Other Volunteers

Many of us will never go serve the needs of others, but we can fund those who do. Whether it is a school for orphans in West Virginia or a Peace Corps project in the West Bank, there are people who want to go serve, and it takes money to finance their lives and travel to make that happen. The people who will uproot their lives to do this type of work amaze me. I have one friend from my early twenties who has been a missionary in Guatemala for twenty-five years or so now. I have others who have gone for a few years and then come back to the States after a few years. All of them are heroes to me. Find some people like this to help and be a part of something that would otherwise be beyond your reach.

Social Entrepreneurship

This is the most encouraging trend in business in our world today. We see a whole class of innovators who are blending traditional capitalism with their passions to do good in the world. They are finding ways to collaborate and effect local economies by creating sustainable businesses that give back or pay forward to their communities by funding public works, bringing new agricultural techniques to third world communities, building or funding schools, or digging wells in arid regions of the globe. The ideas are limitless, and the creativity exhibited to find ways to make a living while doing good are amazing.

Microfunding

This is a new type of funding, enabled by the Internet, that can cut out the middleman and eliminate almost all administrative costs that plague so many charities. My favorite example of microfunding is Kiva.com. On this site you may wholly, or in part, fund an entrepreneur from anywhere in the world. For as little as $25 you can launch a microenterprise in another part of the world. As that business becomes profitable, the entrepreneurs repay the initial investment that was received as a loan. As the money is repaid, it goes back into your Kiva account, allowing you to select another enterprise you would like to help launch. The loan keeps being repaid and goes to fund another start-up, allowing you to multiply your giving exponentially over time.

Some might ask if I am being hypocritical by calling debt *bondage* but then loaning money to people in the third world. I must admit I have struggled with this in principle. In reality what studies have shown is that people have responded better to receiving this hand up, in the form of a loan, rather than a handout, in the form of charity. The perceived value of the money is greater when one has to pay it off out of one's own profits, and the level of responsibility the entrepreneur feels helps him or her push through the difficulties of starting up an enterprise. In addition, the people who repay the loan have a part and take pride in the other ventures that are started from what they repay! It is an ingenious system, and the world is the winner.

Multigenerational Wealth and Giving

We have all read about spoiled trust fund babies and billionaires, like Bill Gates, who are not planning on leaving their fortunes to their children. I am one who believes every situation is different because every child is different. But it is important to point out that the biblical model of a "good man" leaving "an inheritance to his children's children" is still viable today. One case in point is the Cathey family, owners of the fast food empire of Chick-fil-A. They have managed to pass on the ownership effectively to the next generation by working through a detailed succession plan prior to founder Truett Cathey's death.

The reality is that most of us do not have billions to worry about, but if you live out the principles in this book you will be in a position to pass on multigenerational wealth, should you choose to do so. The rules governing taxation of these assets changes continually, so it will be important to work with a financial advisor who also does, or partners with people who do estate planning and even tax planning. Professionals in this arena that know what they are doing will save you far more than the fees they charge. Shop around and make sure you find people who align with your values and have excellent reviews from existing or past clients, and shop also for rates to make sure you are not overpaying.

There are no cookie-cutter solutions for this type of work. You will need to meet with these professionals a few times for them to understand your situation and desires to design a tailored plan for you. If you do not know where to start, I will suggest two organizations that align with my values and have great reviews: Christian Financial Advisors and Kingdom Advisors. Both have experienced estate planners and tax professionals on their teams.

Live

This is one area that we all understand. It takes money to live. This area includes food, shelter, housing, transportation, experiences, and lifestyle. In our society this is the area that is often out of control, causing deficits in the other areas where money is needed. We are encouraged, through nonstop marketing, to have it all now and pay for it later, and then the payments on that indebtedness keep us from moving forward to Financial Freedom.

Guard

We cannot ignore this area. It is insurance. For most of us, we never see a large portion of our pay, because our health, disability, vision, and dental insurances get deducted from our checks. Further, due to large deductibles, we also have money deducted for flexible spending accounts or health savings accounts to pay for those deductibles and out-of-pocket expenses. Add on proper amounts of life insurance to protect your family, and the portion of our budgets required to guard is very significant. Many times, people will skip on this area, especially younger people. To do so is playing with fire, and many, including my father, have suffered financial ruin as a result. In my opinion, this area is not optional. It needs to be a priority in everyone's spending plan.

Owe

The first area in this category is the money we have to direct to pay off *debt*. As we have discussed, to the degree one limits debt, and therefore payments going to debt, the better chances are that one will reach Financial Freedom.

There is another area that is covered in the *owe* category: *taxes!* Everyone loves to hate taxes, and that's OK. Believe me: I get it! We often are frustrated by the inefficiency and ineffectiveness of government programs and government services. Having said that, I know many people who would not hesitate to cheat on their taxes. That is just wrong! Do I think our system of taxation is fair? No! But it is the law of the land, and I enjoy the benefits of living in this land.

No one should pay one more dollar than they owe in taxes.

They should avail themselves of every tax break available in the tax code. This will often necessitate working with a knowledgeable tax professional. On the other hand, no one should pay one dollar less than one owes in taxes either. You *owe* them. You enjoy the benefits of living in the nation, state, county, and city that you do, and therefore, you are obligated to pay the taxes that maintain the infrastructure of the place you live. It is an integrity issue, one that exposes the lack thereof in our societies today. According to CNN Money, $458 billion of taxes goes unpaid every year in the United States alone.

Grow

This is the investing category. It may be investing in yourself through education, investing in your own business, or investing in your 401(k). It is not spending on experiences or stuff. That would fall under the *live* category. The difference in investing and spending is pretty simple. In order to qualify as an investment, there must be a reasonable expectation of a positive financial return over time.

If one wants to win with money and life, he or she has to give, live, guard, and grow, by limiting what he or she must pay on what she owes.

A Note to My Fellow Christians: It Is Good to Win with Money!

For most people this is an obvious statement, but for a lot of people raised in fundamental Christian churches, this statement may make your skin crawl. That was me! I was raised with a belief system that money is evil. I was told you cannot serve God and riches. I thought that having money only leads to temptation. The very story I wrote about earlier—the rich, young ruler who came to Jesus—was used to show it is harder to shove a camel through the eye of a needle than for a rich man to enter heaven. It is right there in red letters (meaning Jesus spoke the words) in my Bible, so it must be true!

Sadly, the rich, young ruler chose his riches over the opportunity of living the life Jesus called him to live. Further, Jesus's comment was meant to shock his disciples who had been brought up with the understanding all through the Old Testament that riches are a sign of God's blessings. He was pointing out that one could pursue the blessings without remembering the giver of all good things.

It is important to note that other rich men in Jesus's life were never called to sell all they have and give to the poor. Matthew, Zacchaeus, Nicodemus, Joseph of Arimathea, and others were men with wealth, and there is no indication that Jesus required this of them. Why not? I think that they had the proper attitude of gratitude when it comes to the blessings God had bestowed and therefore were not called to give it away but rather to continue to manage those blessings for God.

Stewardship

So, if you love riches to the point that you could not give them up to do what God has for you to do, take heed of the camel-and-needle warning. If, however, you recognize that whatever riches you have are actually God's, and you have been called to manage them for His kingdom, then lay aside the guilt and move forward. Pursue your hard work, professionalism, or entrepreneurship, or combination of these, with the knowledge that doing so is every bit as holy an activity as preaching a Sunday sermon from the pulpit or counseling couples who are considering divorce. Use the natural moneymaking, business, and leadership skills God has given you to create wealth, employ others, and deliver products and services to serve others well. Remember that the Bible tells us that a good man leaves an inheritance to his children's children! Leave a legacy filled with purpose and service.

If you still struggle with this concept, there is a class being made available through churches with curriculum developed by author and financial guru Ron Blue called "God Owns It All." It teaches people how to find contentment and confidence in their finances.

Also, the Crown Financial Curriculum, "Managing our Money God's Way," developed by the late, great Larry Burkett is another great resource to get a balanced perspective about the role of money in our lives and our spiritual walk. Finally, Dave Ramsey's *The Legacy Journey* is another must-read on this topic.

The Greatest Legacy of All

You have heard it said many times: When one is on his or her death bed, one will never wish one could have closed that last deal, spent more time at the office, or made more money. When it comes down to it, it just does not matter how much money you made, saved, or spent. Relationships are the real treasures of life. The people with the most joy in life are the ones who are loved well. The ones that are loved well also loved well. Your real legacy will live on in the lives you have touched with your love—your spouse and your kids first, but then the others around you, followed by those who you never even met personally.

There is a great song that tells that story for one man who did not realize the legacy he left until he made it to heaven. It is called "Thank You" by Ray Boltz. It recounts numerous interactions that a man had with people he met in heaven. He came to learn that seemingly mundane activities in his life actually had an eternal effect. One man introduced himself as a boy who the man had taught in Sunday school when he was only eight years old. Another man said he was there because of an offering the man had given one Sunday night when a missionary came to his church and gave a moving presentation of the overseas ministry he represented. On and on, people came to the man to tell him the impact he had on them. Ray put it this way in his lyrics:

> One by one they came
> Far as your eyes could see
> Each life somehow touched
> By your generosity

Little things that you had done
Sacrifices you made
They were unnoticed on the earth
In heaven now proclaimed

Then, in the culmination of the story, he is met by the Savior himself, who compels the man to look upon the many he had impacted and to recognize that they were his reward. His life was filled with meaning because of the relationships he had contributed to, day in and day out, year after year, leaving an eternal legacy in his wake.

CHAPTER 11

It Is Never Too Late!

I was talking to a buddy of mine recently who has a household income that most of us would think is incredible, probably in the $300,000 range. Unfortunately, due to unforeseen circumstances, he is fifty-four years old and had to use all of his retirement savings, so he is starting over on building his nest egg. It was evident in our conversation that he did not think he would be able to build it back up to a million dollars before he retires. His attitude is even more pronounced with others who reach middle age and have not concentrated on retirement savings and do not make a salary that high. I am here to tell you that assumption is probably not valid, and the table below will demonstrate why I think that is true. So for all of you who are fifty-something and think it is too late, take a look at this analysis, and hopefully, it will help you have hope for your financial future.

Let me orient you to the chart. It is set up so that you can look at the row with your current retirement savings and the column with your current income level, find where the two intersect and see how many years it will take you to amass $1 million. I assumed that you will invest 15 percent of your income, and that you will average 10 percent returns, which is in line with historical performance of the stock market as is evidenced by the S&P 500 index since 1929. Current median household income in the US is about $50,000, and as we are talking about people who are experienced and usually at higher end of the income spectrum, I have started the chart at that level. If you do fall below the $50,000 mark, work on that element first because you will need to in order become a millionaire. If you have less than $100,000 in savings you will need one to five years longer to get to the $1 million mark, but this table will likely apply to the 80 percent of you who are in your fifties and are not even halfway to the million mark, and hopefully show you *can* get there!

Hope For Procrastinators

Current Retirement Savings	Household Income										
	$50,000	$75,000	$100,000	$125,000	$150,000	$175,000	$200,000	$225,000	$250,000	$275,000	$300,000
$100,000	20 yrs	18 yrs	17 yrs	15 yrs	14 yrs	14 yrs	13 yrs	12 yrs	12 yrs	11 yrs	11 yrs
$150,000	17 yrs	16 yrs	15 yrs	14 yrs	13 yrs	12 yrs	12 yrs	11 yrs	11 yrs	10 yrs	10 yrs
$200,000	15 yrs	14 yrs	13 yrs	12 yrs	12 yrs	11 yrs	11 yrs	10 yrs	10 yrs	9 yrs	9 yrs
$250,000	13 yrs	12 yrs	12 yrs	11 yrs	10 yrs	10 yrs	10 yrs	9 yrs	9 yrs	8 yrs	8 yrs
$300,000	12 yrs	11 yrs	10 yrs	10 yrs	9 yrs	9 yrs	9 yrs	8 yrs	8 yrs	8 yrs	7 yrs
$350,000	10 yrs	10 yrs	9 yrs	9 yrs	8 yrs	8 yrs	8 yrs	7 yrs	7 yrs	7 yrs	7 yrs
$400,000	9 yrs	9 yrs	8 yrs	8 yrs	8 yrs	7 yrs	7 yrs	7 yrs	7 yrs	6 yrs	6 yrs
$450,000	8 yrs	8 yrs	7 yrs	7 yrs	7 yrs	7 yrs	6 yrs	6 yrs	6 yrs	6 yrs	6 yrs
$500,000	7 yrs	7 yrs	6 yrs	6 yrs	6 yrs	6 yrs	6 yrs	5 yrs	5 yrs	5 yrs	5 yrs

ASSUMPTIONS
15% of income going into Retirment Savings
10% avg annual return on Investments

Let's look at my buddy first. I am pretty sure that his wife has retirement savings, so let's assume that is $100,000 and look at the intersection of that and his $300,000 salary. As you can see, based on the assumptions, he should reach $1 million in 11 years. This means he can probably retire at age 65 with $1 million.

I know what you're thinking: "OK, but that is a guy making $300,000!" You are right, so let's talk about a fifty-year-old guy who is making $50,000 and has only saved $100,000 thus far. Even this guy can retire at seventy (twenty years from today) with $1 million in retirement! Where do you fall? Can you commit to save 15 percent of your salary if it means you will have financial freedom in 20 years or less? While there are no guarantees, I hope that you can see from this illustration that it is not too late for you to achieve a meaningful level of retirement savings if you will commit to take consistent action starting today. Intentionality and delayed gratification are all that is required for most of us, at any age, to be millionaires!

If you would like to get your exact projection, I used the retirement calculator at Bankrate.com. You can enter a few elements and get a good quick picture of what your retirement picture looks like. It will help you see whether you will need to slash lifestyle, work longer, or increase your annual savings to sustain yourself in retirement. As I stated earlier, I recommend the help of a good financial planner to help you do a deep dive, but this and other similar tools are great for a first look.

So the decision is now up to you. Do you hear a sound in the distance? It is the sound of your train. It is getting ready to leave the station. I hear it calling, "I think you can. I think you can. I think you can!" The conductor has returned to lead you out of Normal. You are his number ten. He is waiting, but he cannot wait forever. Time is growing shorter each passing day, so do not delay!

Another Journey Starts

*Then one day as you are driving home, you hear this guy on the radio talking about erasing debt from your life. He tells you that it is time to have a **Total Money Make Over**, so you can have **Financial Peace** in your life. You hear these families who come into his radio studio and tell their stories of how they got out of tens, or even hundreds of thousands in debt! A flip switches inside you. You have had it! You cannot live in bondage anymore. You have determined you are leaving Normal. You are getting out of debt and starting your journey to Financial Freedom!*

*You go home and tell your wife and the kids that you are starting on a new journey. You explain to them that you will have to make some sacrifices. For a time, you will have to "live like no one else, so that later you can live and give like no one else." You explain that you now see a way to have a life with **No More Dreaded Mondays** because you are ready to live out your calling where **Wisdom Meets Passion**. For a time, you may have to live on "beans and rice," but soon people would*

See You at the Top. *You now believe it is not too late to **Master Your Money after the Big 5-0** and that you want to live out the example so that you can **Raise Money-Smart Kids** and **Build Wealth That Lasts and have a Home Run Life.***

Your wife looks at you and says, "I am not sure what has happened, but we will do whatever it takes. What do we need to do?"

"Pack your bags for a long journey," you answer. "We have to get to the train station."

CHAPTER 12

It Is Time for Your Journey!

You and your family arrive breathless at the train station on Hope Hill, prepared for the journey. You look around at an amazing sight. You are in the hub of a labyrinth of tunnels, tracks, and elevated tracks. There are platforms with people waiting everywhere you turn, with stairs and escalators and halls extending as far as you can see in every direction. You see a crowd gathered around a pillar in the center of the station, and you make your way toward the strange obelisk. As you approach, you see that the people gathered are of all sorts. You observe young and old, well dressed to vagrants, all races, and from their attire, apparently many different religions and cultures. Some of them are moving frantically from one of the four sides of the pillar to the other, then the other, while others seemed to be standing transfixed, and yet others, lost and dismayed. You see two men, one older and one your age, and one woman dressed in conductor's attire, and you walk up to them and ask them for help. The older conductor informs you that this is the station map that you may use to find the right track to take you on your journey.

"I am looking for the track to Millionaire Mountain," you say. "Can you tell me which track goes there?"

The older man turns to the younger man and the woman, and gestures to them saying, "Why certainly. All of these tracks could eventually lead to Millionaire Mountain, but you have to find the *right track for you. These two conductors will be happy to help you find the right track for you!"*

"I don't understand," you reply. "What do you mean, the right track for me?"

The woman answers saying, "If you have arrived here, it is because you understand there is something more out there than Normal. Deep inside, you want to be more than you can be in Normal, and do more than you can do in Normal. This place was designed to help you find the right track, for you, to make the journey that only you can make."

Your wife replies, "That is exactly why we are here! Please show us the way."

"We would be happy to," says the younger male conductor who is obviously the husband of the female conductor as they start walking hand in hand toward one of the tunnels.

Your whole family follows the two conductors that are similar in age to you, leaving the older conductor by the pillar. You look back and see a frantic young man run up to him. The older conductor places a hand on his shoulder, calming him instantly as he explains to him that he is in the right place and that he is right on time. It occurs to you what a great job these conductors have!

Are You Ready to Start Your Journey?

If so, take leadership guru Stephen Covey's advice and "begin with the end in mind!" Renowned speaker and life coach, Kent Juilan, recently led a group of us through a process in his "Live It Forward—Advance" conference that helped us do just that. I hope you find it valuable as well.

X Marks the Spot—What Is Your Treasure?

Imagine that life is an elaborate treasure hunt, and you have been handed a treasure map to guide you to the prize. On that map, there is an X. That is the place to where you are trying to get, the place where all your dreams come true. A map without the X is useless. You have to find your X.

Here are a couple of exercises to help you:

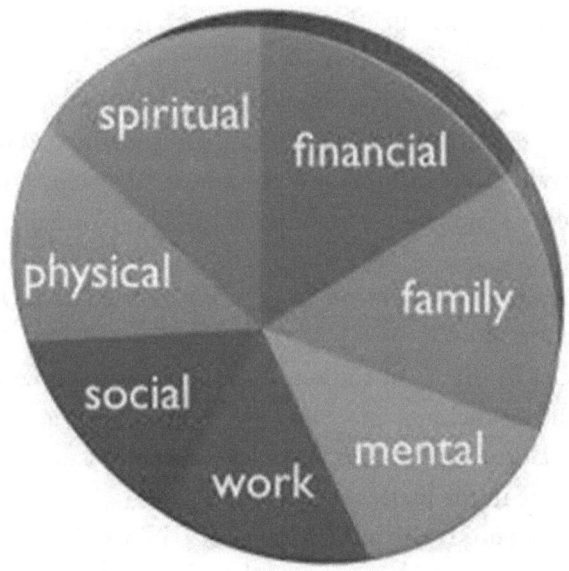

1. Remember Zig Ziglar's "Wheel of Life"? Let's use it again to help you set your compass for this journey. Take an hour or two and think about what winning means to you? Write down what you think your ultimate goals are in each of the seven areas listed above. If you are married, have your spouse do the same and compare the results. Talk about any areas that look different and find a way to get to a shared vision.
2. If that approach is too structured, try this one. Answer the question: "What do I want others to say about me at my funeral?" Write your own eulogy! That will tell you what truly is most important to you at your core.
3. If you would like extra credit, do both. The compelling vision you create will help you focus on the things that really matter.

You Are Ready to Ride!

Now you have clarity on where your X is. Let that guide you on your next step, then the next leg of the journey, and ultimately it will lead you to exactly where you want to go. Check in on this every couple of years, because the farther you move in your journey, the clearer your X becomes.

Now that you have your map in hand, I believe you are ready to make your journey. I think you can! Do you? If so, start today! Do not wait! Every day counts! Remember the steps to make it successfully so you will not end up returning to Normal!

1. **Make up your mind to go**: Think for yourself. Don't be normal!
2. **Get to the train station**: Take only what you need. Leave the rest behind!
3. **Pick the right track**: Three-legged stool: passion, skills, and value in the marketplace.
4. **Pick your train:** Job Train, Career Train, or Entrepreneurial Express?
5. **Fuel the engine:** Invest continuously to keep the train moving.
6. **Look at the landscape:** Enjoy the ride, find new opportunities, and explore the world.
7. **Leave a legacy**: Impact the world by leading and giving.

I wish you well on your journey. I look forward to seeing you on the top of Millionaire Mountain or in the land of Financial Freedom beyond!

EPILOGUE

A Thank You to the "Conductors" in My Life

Larry Burkett and Ron Blue

I am so grateful for my many mentors who have guided me on my journey to Financial Freedom. It all began with the work of a man named Larry Burkett, who had a radio show in the 1980s and 1990s called "Money Matters," produced by his company, Christian Financial Concepts. I lived in Atlanta at the time as did he, and I really liked what he had to say but implemented little of it at first. Later, I had a young, married couples Sunday school class that used his curriculum. I am not even certain what it was called. It might have been "The Complete Financial Guide for Young Couples," but I am not certain. What I am certain about was that my wife and I took away three important skills and practices from that class that we implemented from that point on in our lives, and I believe they were the foundation to our financial success. They are the following:

1. **Budgeting:** Nothing you can learn in personal finance is more important than this skill and practice. Learning how to tell your money where to go instead of wondering where it went is the single, most important factor for financial success. Doing it together, as a couple, may be the single,

most important thing couples can do to be on the same page about all of their priorities in life.

2. **Cash Envelopes:** Once you have a budget, using cash envelopes for things that you do not routinely pay online, at set times of the month (like rent, mortgage, and utilities), is a great practice. Use cash envelopes for things like groceries, entertainment, gasoline, clothes. When you get to the last week of the month, and there is no money in the restaurant envelope, it is time to eat at home. We also use it to save all year for things like car tags, home owners association fees, car repairs, and vacation, so the money would be there when we needed it and we were not "surprised." Some banks have come up with virtual cash envelopes within a checking account. This is an option, but remember that spending with cash has been proven to elicit an emotional response that can be dulled by the use of electronic payment. I encourage you to use real, paper money. It will help you spend less.

3. **Retirement Saving/Investing:** We started very slowly in this endeavor at 4 percent, because that was all we believed we could do, but my very wise wife said we needed to increase every year out of our raises. We did that, sometimes only going up 1 percent per year, until a few years later we reached our goal of 10 percent. Later we increased that to 15 percent

I should also mention that we became committed to tithing, giving 10 percent of our income to Christian ministry, through Larry's teaching. We had tried in the past, but at this stage, it became a firm commitment. *Generous living* is an important part of Larry's teaching, laid out in a book by one of Larry's partners in ministry, Ron Blue. They wrote books together and separately through the years until Mr. Burkett went home to be with Jesus in 2003. Mr. Blue continues to take the message of financial stewardship to the church through his organization of financial advisors, Kingdom

Advisors, books, and a brand-new curriculum for small groups called "God Owns It All." All of their writings are extremely valuable, especially for Christians seeking to get a handle on what place money has in the life of a Christian.

Zig Ziglar

I cannot tell you what an impact this man had on my life. He is well known as a motivational guru. Like Larry Burkett, he was an outspoken Christian, and he too has gone on to heaven ahead of us, but his homespun humor and positive message attracted people from every race, religion, and creed. For me, it had the most impact on my career. In my thirties, I finally graduated with my MBA, which I had secured going to school full-time while working three jobs. When I got the degree and we had our first son, nothing seemed to happen in my career for over a year. I started listening to Zig Ziglar tapes and reading his books at this time, and his encouragement led to hope and belief in my ability to succeed in my career. A year later I took a very risky job as a rural hospital CEO. Fortunately, things went well and it launched me into a new level of executive leadership in healthcare, which has given me meaningful work while providing well for my family and our future.

Dave Ramsey

About nine years ago I saw a bald guy on a billboard with the caption "Act Your Wage!" and a local radio station and times for the "Dave Ramsey Show." I tuned in and started listening, and I was hooked. His commonsense, "Baby Step" approach to personal finance was the simplest, most succinct explanation I had ever heard. Of course, I just listened and agreed with everything because I had my act together, or did I? I began hearing about people who not only had eliminated credit card and school loans like I did, but also owned their cars and even their homes! I had just financed $19,500 on a used SUV, and did not even have enough equity in my house to avoid private mortgage insurance. My 403(b) was healthy, and we were contributing 10 percent per year, but this guy said I should be doing 15 percent. I decided I would pick up his new book, *The Total Money Makeover*. My wife and I read it in a few days.

The material was great, but the stories of people who had paid off massive amounts of debt in a year, or two or three, were astounding and inspiring. Then there were the people who had actually paid off their houses! This hit home with me so hard, probably because we had lost our home to bankruptcy when I was eleven years old.

At that time there was a change in leadership at my hospital, and though I weathered the storm and came out whole, I had several friends who did not. I thought, "If I own my home, I could survive anything like that in the future, but as long as I have that mortgage payment, I am vulnerable." My wife and I started our total money makeover, and seven years later, we paid off our mortgage! We are coming up on our two-year anniversary of being 100 percent debt-free, and I cannot describe the difference it is making in our life.

I have found this arena so exciting that I have started informally doing some financial coaching, and I have coordinated three financial peace classes at my church. I have seen people grab hold of these principles and take control of their lives and money. I highly recommend the materials from Ramsey Solutions for anyone. Chris Hogan's *Retire Inspired* is a great tool for helping you get your retirement squared away. The "Generation Change" material is great for teens, especially as they are looking at how to get to college without taking on a mountain of debt. Dave's book *EntreLeadership* is a great book on starting and running a small business, and his book he wrote with his daughter, Rachel Cruz, *Smart Money, Smart Kids,* rivals Ron and Judy Blue's book *Raising Money-Smart Kids* as the definitive work on this topic.

Thomas J. Stanley, PhD

The Millionaire Next Door and *The Millionaire Mind* author's research and writing solidified my belief that the plan I was working could and would lead me to financial freedom. He showed me that most millionaires were men and women just like me. They worked hard, lived on less than they made, and delayed gratification to reach their higher goals and purpose. His work inspired me and put in me a desire to achieve my dream so that I might inspire others to achieve theirs.

Dan Miller

I got acquainted with Dan and his book *48 Days to the Work You Love* through Dave Ramsey. He often gives away this book to people whose financial crisis is a result of an income or career crisis. I started listening to Dan's *48 Days* weekly podcast. The podcast intrigued me, because it drew me into a community of people who have taken their wisdom and passion into the marketplace and created businesses that offered them a lot more freedom and a lot more income than they had achieved in their regular jobs or careers. As I was turning fifty at the time, I decided I would get the *48 Days* book and go through the process myself. In my case, I determined that my current career path in healthcare administration was aligned with my wisdom and passion, and I decided to take on a new role in a larger organization with greater challenges, so I could have greater impact.

I believe that may change in the future and that I may indeed embark on a second-act career in personal finance and career coaching. If you are contemplating such a move, I highly recommend Dan's book that he coauthored with his son, Jared, *Wisdom Meets Passion*, and go through the step-by-step process outlined in *48 Days to the Work You Love*.

Kevin Myers

Pastor Kevin Myers, or "PK" as we affectionately refer to him, is the senior pastor of 12Stone Church. It is one church in many locations throughout metro Atlanta and online. He has coauthored a great book along with John Maxwell, titled, *Home Run Life*. The teaching in this book is the core teaching of 12Stone, using a baseball diamond to help us prioritize things in our lives so that we can be what God has called us to be and that God can get the glory. If you would like to get a synopsis of the book, check out my blog post from my blog at 3rsofsuccess.com. Here is the direct link for your convenience: http://wp.me/p3evWc-aX.

www.ingramcontent.com/pod-product-compliance
Lightning Source LLC
Chambersburg PA
CBHW030744180526
45163CB00003B/913